Power Through Prayer

Power Through Prayer

Rev. Dr. B.J. Sands

POWER THROUGH POWER

Intentional • Connectional • Inspirational

Prayers to God

with

Rev. Dr. B. J. Sands

POWER THROUGH POWER

is dedicated to my parents,
Mrs. Helen Corpening Phillips,
Mr. Arthrow Phifer Perkins
Mr. C. O. Phillips,
their parents, grandparents,
and ancestors, who made sacrifices,
kept the faith and paved the way for me.

CONTENTS

POWER THROUGH POWER

FOREWORD

You hold in your hand the acceptance of an invitation to join Rev. Dr. Barbara Sands in her prayer closet during a defined season in her life. It provides the opportunity for you to reflect on the commonality of your experiences with this Woman of God. Over the fifty-two years of our friendship, Barbara and I have shared as professionals, parents, activists, and more recently as co-authors in "Bringing Into Being Our Legacy." Barbara Sands accepted God's call in this tremulous moment in the world to share her Prayers to God to encourage others to communicate with God more freely.

As our environment challenges us, prayer will center us inward to the Peace of God within us that transcends all human understanding. "Power Through Prayer" enlarges our prayer life by reminding us of the diversity of creation and our abundance: sunlight, moonlight, water, land, vegetation, stars, and living creatures.

With a Sense of Gratitude, I Congratulate My Beloved Friend and encourage readers to share *"Power Through Prayer"* with family, friends, and anyone experiencing an exceptionally challenging time.

Blessings,

Dr. Salima Marriott

October 14, 2024

POWER THROUGH POWER

ACKNOWLEDGMENTS

My sincere gratitude to:

My beloved husband and best friend, Rev. Dr. Douglas B. Sands, Sr., is always here. His love and guidance helped me birth this book. He is my best supporter and critic; He gave me the time to write my book and encouraged me to stay on track.

My daughter, by love, LaTasha McKinney, my Technical Guru and Website Designer, for loving, encouraging, and challenging me to do more. For rearranging her schedule without me knowing it needed adjustment. For her gentleness as she chastises me for not meeting her schedule. For her research ability and her thoroughness in any project she tackles on my behalf.

Dr. Salima Marriott, my life coach, mentor, and friend-sister, for her many years of helping me be the best and to remain focused. She invited me to be a contributing author to her book *"Bringing Into Being Our Legacy."* Dr. Marriott also directed me to Melanie Bonita Kelly, who leads the Daily Dose of Prayer Collaboration.

My grandson, Douglas Bruce Sands, III, is a critical thinker-analyzer who always loves and encourages me. He has a wealth of suggestions to make my life easier and is always available to assist with any project.

Ms. Cheryl Miles has the prettiest smile and a great personality. She has great patience with me. I thank her for her creativity. She is a designer of books, covers, bulletins, and cards. Cheryl has great technological and organizational skills.

Brother James Thomas Beal for his patience as he works with me through YouTube, Microsoft 365, and Zoom Workplace. He has the patience of Job; he spent many hours with me trying to make clear what I am trying to accomplish using the computer. He is very knowledgeable and navigates through this technology quietly and slowly with me.

Brother Julian Henson, Tournament and Event Supervisor and Marketing Consultant, for his patience, talent, skills, and wisdom in working with the author.

Joan Manley, Editor, for her love, support, and prayers for the author and this project.

POWER THROUGH POWER

INTRODUCTION

Prayer expresses the deepest desires of the human heart and the highest joy of the soul. Prayer seeks beyond the mysteries of the believer's relationship with God. Prayer is the measure of Trust, the essence of Faith, and the hope of Obedience.

Prayer is each believer's own sacred act of communing with God. Prayer is a holy privilege as a gift of Grace for each and every soul to receive the Presence, the Power, and the Authority of God to bless their lives.

Here in *"Power Through Prayer,"* we will experience the actual moving of the soul in the rapture of a believer's prayers in common, ordinary, everyday life and in extremely challenging times of need.

Drawing from a lifetime of faith and experience, my wife offers prayers that resonate with the human heart. This collection reflects her unwavering belief in the transformative power of prayer.

May you be blessed through the Power of the Holy Spirit with God's answers to your prayers. May you be blessed through the Power of the Holy Spirit with a closer Relationship with God.

Rev. Dr. Douglas B. Sands, Sr.
October 15, 2024

HOLY SCRIPTURE

POWER THROUGH POWER

HOLY SCRIPTURE

For it is God who works in you both to will and
to do for His good pleasure.
Do all things without complaining and disputing,
that you may become blameless and harmless,
children of God without fault in the midst of a
crooked and perverse generation, among whom
you shine as lights in the world.

Phil. 2:13-15 (NKJV)

1

CHRISTIANITY - A WAY OF LIFE

A CHANGE IS COMING

Be still, and know that I am God; I will be exalted among the nations, I will be exalted in the earth! ~ Ps. 46:10 (NKJV)

Holy, Righteous God of the universe, I thank You for the rains that water the earth. I praise You for the beauty of creation. I honor You for Your wisdom, knowledge, love, and devotion to humankind. Your Majesty fills the creation. Your footsteps carve out the direction for us to follow You.

Thank You, Father, for watching and keeping us on the right path. The world needs a change, Father. Men are following the Antichrist and have lost their ability to examine and find themselves approved. They would rather live in a world that has lost its integrity. Morality and ethics are at the lowest level of attention. Few seem to want to be decent, loving, kind, generous, compassionate, and patient with other people. I know You are watching and caring for each one of us. I believe that You will bring a change to this world.

Creating God, our children are watching and are lost. Strengthen us to watch, pray, and turn from the Antichrist, who is out to destroy us all. Open our hearts to return to You, pray, abstain from wrongdoing, and seek Your way. You told us we would hear from You. A change must come, Father.

In the name of Jesus. Amen.

A HUMBLE HEART

Therefore humble yourselves under the mighty hand of God, that He may exalt you in due time, ~ 1 Pet. 5:6 (NKJV)

Father God, please give me a humble heart. I want to serve You as You deserve, for You are the great, holy, and mighty God. I want to please You in all that I do, that I may cause You no disturbance in Your Spirit, no heartache over any actions that I may commit. My soul, my body belong to You. I am Yours. Do with me what You will. You are my God, my Father, my Friend, my Healer, my Deliverer, my constant help in the time of trouble. You are my everything.

Thank You, God, for blessing my family; my husband, children, grandchildren, great-grandchildren, nieces, nephews, cousins, aunts, uncles, and everybody around the globe. Thank You for my big family. May I never forget that I am one of many generations that have lived a life, fought the fight, and remained faithful to You. I must follow in my ancestors' footsteps. May I please You, God, to the utmost.

In the name of Jesus, I pray. Amen.

BEING A CHRISTIAN

With my whole heart I have sought You; Oh, let me not wander from Your commandments! ~ Ps. 119:10 (NKJV)

Holy Father of the Universe, greetings to You this beautiful morning. Father, thank You for allowing me to be one of Your children. Thank You for holding me in the palm of Your hand. Thank You for allowing me to share in Your goodness. Thank You for making me ever so conscious of my responsibilities as a believer in You. Thank You for allowing me to love my sisters and brothers as I love myself. Thank You, Father, for leading me to strive for consistency in my discipline, so that I may stay connected to You. Being a believer is not a program that we follow; it is a way of life. As a believer in the Living God, I find hope through Jesus Christ and the presence of the Holy Spirit to be a way of life. Thank You, God, for allowing me to be a Christian, striving to please and honor You, and for being supportive of my sisters and brothers around the globe. Thank You for the Christian Way of life.

In the name of Jesus, I pray. Amen.

COURAGE AND THE WORDS TO SPEAK

for it is not you who speak, but the Spirit of your Father who speaks in you. ~ Matt. 10:20 (NKJV)

Father, it has been a mighty good day. We worshiped using the virtual platform due to problems with the air conditioner in the House of Prayer. Father, You spoke to us through the praise songs, and Your Spirit was high. We felt the presence of the Lord, and we were going to get our blessing. You spoke to us, Father, through the prayers and the testimonies. Your Spirit, presence, and power filled the homes of each person through ZOOM. Thank You, Father, for speaking through me today and reminding the sisters and brothers of the way we must share our faith stories with others. Our sharing will encourage them and remind them that You are always on time. Always listening to us and for us to come to You and to have faith in You. You will not tarry long.

In Jesus' name. Amen.

EARTHLY GAINS OVER ETERNAL LIFE

Fight the good fight of faith, lay hold on eternal life, to which you were also called and have confessed the good confession in the presence of many witnesses. ~ 1 Tim. 6:12 (NKJV)

Forgiving God of all creation, Life Sustainer, and Friend; Thank You for never leaving us to our own devices for long. Satan is attacking Your children every day. Enticing them to choose earthly gains and not cling to You. We would rather have fun, be popular, have a lot of friends, and participate in things ungodly than look to the One who offers us eternal life. Satan wants us to choose a fast car, a big house in a great neighborhood, lots of clothes, purchase tickets to the ballgames, see the Hollywood stars, cheat on our taxes, try to cheat God, and even abort life to fulfill our wants and desires.

Create in us a clean heart so that we may realize that earthly gains are temporary, and the joys are short-lived. Remind us that we have a Savior who promised us eternal life and everlasting joy.

In Jesus' name, we pray. Amen.

JUSTICE FOR WOMEN

He shall bring forth your righteousness as the light, And your justice as the noonday. ~ Ps. 37:6 (NKJV)

Lord, thank You for another opportunity to make a difference in the universe. You are the One who blesses us when we don't realize we have been blessed. Thank You, Lord, for using another sister to help us reach more people through the stories of 16 black women. They are engaged in the struggle for justice for women worldwide. Thank you for allowing us to use our experiences and knowledge to free those who are younger, encouraging them to be strong, truthful, and forthright in speaking out against injustices perpetrated upon women by those who would degrade, dehumanize, and physically, emotionally, and verbally abuse them. Thank You, Lord, for the Doni Glover Radio Program. We were interviewed and received information to share with others.

In the name of Jesus. Amen.

KEEPING CENTERED

Let each of you look out not only for his own interests, but also for the interests of others. ~ Phil. 2:4 (NKJV)

Father of the universe, who knows all about being centered and keeping balanced in life, I am seeking Your perfect balance. Thank You for keeping me away from the extreme left (being so heavenly-minded that I am no earthly good;) or to the extreme right (being so earthly-minded that I laugh at those who believe in You). Thank You for re-minding me that all souls are Yours, and that we are one family in Christ. Thank You for helping me keep the main thing, *the main thing*, being centered on Christ.

In His name, I pray. Amen.

KEEPING HIS COMMANDMENTS

And whatever we ask we receive from Him, because we keep His com-mandments and do those things that are pleasing in His sight. ~ 1 John 3:22 (NKJV)

Lord, I thank You for Your favor. You hear the cries of Your children. When we yield to temptations, we are mindful of how displeased You are with us and our behavior. You talk to us in our hearts, and we yearn to correct what was done. We pray to You, and You lead us to repen-tance. Lord, I thank You. We long to do right, and our sin is ever before us. You, O Lord, know our hearts, and You continue to talk to us and encourage us to be strong, speak to the situation, make restitution, accept Your forgiveness, and forgive ourselves.

Your love never fails. Thank You, Father, for loving me despite my failure. You know my heart. You know me. Thank You for always being with me. Thank You for salvation.

In the name of Jesus. Amen.

KEEPING YOU IN MY PRAYERS

For God is my witness, whom I serve [a] with my spirit in the gospel of His Son, that without ceasing I make mention of you always in my prayers, ~ Rom. 1:9 (NKJV)

Lord of Hosts, to You, I raise my prayers of thankful praise for my sisters and brothers in the world today. I thank You, God, for those who are in foreign countries. Thank You for those who are in the United States. Thank You for everyone, dear God, regardless of their nationality, color, creed, or race. I believe, Father, You created us to be sisters and brothers, and to love each other unconditionally. I further believe that recognizing diversity leads us to understand and respect each other more fully. It calls on us to not only be united, but to appreciate the differences as we listen, exercise patience, and kindness as we work together. When all the parts work together harmoniously, it benefits everyone.

My heart is grateful, dear God, as I continue to pray daily for my sisters and brothers nearby and those around the world. We are one in the Spirit, one in Christ, and one in You.

In Jesus' name, I pray. Amen.

MOISTURIZING CREAM

I beseech you therefore, brethren, by the mercies of God, that you present your bodies a living sacrifice, holy, acceptable to God, which is your reasonable service. ~ Rom. 12:1 (NKJV)

Thank You, Father God, for providing Absolute Moisturizing Cream for my face. This cream is lovely and smooth, and it does exactly what it claims on the label. Thank You for giving me the funds to be able to purchase this cream. You revealed to me what I needed for my face. But then, God, thank You for giving me all that I need for moisturizing my body, cleansing, polishing, lubricating, smoothing, and removing dry skin, as well as preventing hair breakage. You provide everything I need for total body upkeep. I praise Your name, and I thank You for all You do for me. Allow me, O God, to share the good news about You with other women, so they may find the solutions that are helpful to them. Thank You for Your wisdom and Your guidance. Every blessing You give me is a gift of Your love.

In Jesus' name, I pray. Amen.

LORD KEEP ME FOCUSED, PLEASE

As Jesus passed on from there, He saw a man named Matthew sitting at the tax office. And He said to him, "Follow Me." So he arose and followed Him. ~ Matt. 9:9 (NKJV)

Thank You for being my God, *deliverer*, *shield*, and my *buckler*. Thank You for keeping my mind on You. Thank You for Your strength to continue to work on the manuscripts so they can be completed.

Thank You, Lord, for all You have done for me and my family. Keep things that are not of You out of my mind. Keep my heart pure of vile thoughts or ideas. Keep my hands doing as You would have me do and my feet walking forward on the path of righteousness. Keep my eyes fixed on You. Keep my thoughts focused on things that are not of this world. Keep me doing what You would have me do for my siblings.

Thank You for allowing us to travel together up the King's Highway. Thank You for keeping me grounded, remembering that there are no big I's and little u's. You are the King of my life. I love You, Lord. I honor You. Thank You for keeping me focused.

In the name of Jesus. Amen.

NEW BEGINNINGS

They are new every morning; Great is Your faithfulness.
~ Lam. 3:23 (NKJV)

Father God, thank You for Your tender mercies and faithfulness. I reflect on the doubts and fears I had yesterday. I think about all the problems that flood our souls: racial tensions, deceitfulness, separations in families, jealousies between people of all ages, and anger about something that occurred generations ago. People are often overwhelmed by past events they don't understand, events that occurred to them that they wish had not happened. I know that only You, Father, can clarify or fix it so we can move forward in the name of Jesus. We want a new beginning, Father, if it is in Your plan. Your faithfulness is new every morning. Every morning, You wake me to a new day, which I see as a new beginning – a new opportunity to get it right, to do better today than I did yesterday. Thank You, Father, for new beginnings, filled with love, grace, and mercy.

In the name of Jesus. Amen.

NO OFFENSE AGAINST YOU, FATHER

This being so, I myself always strive to have a conscience without of-
fense toward God and men. ~ Acts 24:16 (NKJV)

O Lord, my God, I love You and I honor You. My sincere desire is to please You in my daily living. My intent is never to cause You any heartache, pain, or displeasure. Father, cleave my tongue to the roof of my mouth when I hear something that I know is a falsehood against one of Your children. Thank You for granting me wisdom today, to think, say a silent prayer, then speak to the situation and the person in love, filled with kindness, grace, and mercy. Father, keep me ever so mindful that if I offend any of my sisters and brothers, I offend You. Strengthen me, Father, to not offend You or others.

In the name of Jesus. Amen.

OLD WOMEN NEED YOUNG WOMEN

And on My menservants and on My maidservants I will pour out My Spirit in those days; And they shall prophesy. *~ Acts 2:18 (NKJV)*

Lord of my life, You sent a great blessing my way today. I needed to do some shopping for my great-grandchildren. I realize, Father, that I am not in tune with the young children of today. Their likes are different from mine. I selected some items and was just moving along, shopping, and enjoying my life. God, I thank You for sending this young mother, about 28-30 years old, with two children. She, too, was shopping. I stopped her and showed her my items. She thought they were nice. I asked her if she thought my great-grandchildren would like them. She asked their ages. I told her. She stated her kids were six and eight years old. She asked them if they liked these things. They liked 6 of the 10 items. They selected a different jacket for my little great-grandson. I told her how helpful she was to me. She was glad to be of help. She stated to me, "One day I will be your age. I hope someone will be there to help me. I hope I can be as loving and kind as you are." We hugged, two sisters, two strangers, black and white, that You put together for a moment, Father, to show love, compassion, grace, and mercy.

In Jesus' name. Amen.

PATH DIRECTING GOD

In all your ways acknowledge Him, And He shall direct your paths. ~ Prov. 3:6 (NKJV)

God of possibilities, God of solutions that seem insurmountable, God who never fails, God who has the who, what, when, and where, while we are trying to figure it out. I honor You and praise Your name. Father, the time has come for downsizing. My husband of 51 years and I have approximately 280 books in this house. We were trying to figure out what to do with all these books. Father, we decided to invite young Preachers to come for lunch and look at the books, deciding which ones they might want or need.

Thank You, God, for always being in the plan. One of the Preachers is serving on the Prison Reform Commission. They aim to establish a library for people who are released and provide them with reading materials to help them pursue their interests. When he saw the books, his heart leaped with joy. Lord, You always know what is best for Your children. The Preachers took about 125 books out today. We will be able to donate the remaining books in honor of the One in Christ Preachers Hall of Fame. I prayed, Lord, and You answered. You again provided the solution to the problem that we could not solve. Thank You, Father, You did it again.

In Jesus' name. Amen.

RACISM ALIVE AND THRIVING

Oh, that men would give thanks to the Lord for His goodness, And for His wonderful works to the children of men! ~ Ps. 107:8 (NKJV)

Father, thank You for being a just and impartial God! You know me so well. Today, You, Father, had my tongue cleave to the roof of my mouth. You blessed me with a great periodontal report and a wonderful lunch with my husband. I received telephone calls from each of my children and a surprise visit from one of my granddaughters. It was a peaceful, quiet, God-filled day.

At the restaurant, the young, white waitress, who was approximately 15 years old, was incredibly sweet and patient. It was too hot to eat outside, which was our plan. She took us inside, walked past three available tables, and led us into a space in the rear of the restaurant. I immediately stated, "We are not sitting here. Take us to the front so we can sit at one of the available tables that we just passed." She replied, "Yes, ma'am." She was not aware of what she had just done. Lord, she is a product of her environment. She was just as pleasant as she could be. Father, thank You for the experience today. We must continue to bring everything before You in prayer. Pray for the young lady's enlightenment, Father. I pray that we may all be more mindful and considerate in our actions. We must always represent You. It is a way of life with our sisters and brothers on the journey.

In Jesus' name. Amen.

RACISM IS TAUGHT TO CHILDREN

Therefore let him who thinks he stands take heed lest he fall.
~ 1 Cor. 10:12 (NKJV)

My Father and my God, the Keeper of my soul, my strong Tower, You are my strength when I am weak. When I see others belittling Your followers, trying to turn them away from You and lead them to follow the enemy, and when sisters conspire against each other, it causes pain in my heart. When brothers are testing their strength in jest, and suddenly the enemy emerges, only to destroy a life, it makes me wonder why they do not value life. When little children, black and white, boys and girls, hugging and loving each other, and the next day say, "I can play with you here at school, but not when we are out of school," I know racism is taught at home. When a little white child says on Wednesday, "You are my best friend," to a little black child, go home and return to school on Thursday and say, "We can be friendly at school, but you cannot be my best friend, because you are black," I am convinced that their parents do not understand Your *word*. These are actions that are trying to conquer my soul. Do not let the enemy bring me down. Help me to remember Your *word*. Help me to teach Your *word*, help me to make a difference each day. Help me to stand, Father.

In Jesus' name. Amen.

RECEIVE AND WALK

As you therefore have received Christ Jesus the Lord, so walk in Him,
~ Col. 2:6 (NKJV)

Lord, King of my life, You are the Beginning and the End of everything. You are the Master Ruler of heaven and earth. I love You, Lord, since the beginning of my time. Elders taught me from the cradle about You and Your constant presence in our lives. They taught me that You see everything and know every thought that I have before I know it. Goodness, kindness, love, and truthfulness are what You require of me. Lord, I received what they put into me. Please help me pass it on to my great-grandchildren. If you believe it, then you can live it.

The walk with You is not easy. Walking in, You must come from deep within our soul. We must desire to walk with You and trust in You because we know in our hearts that it is the right thing to do. When we receive Christ Jesus the Lord, there is joy.

In Jesus' name. Amen.

SENIOR OLYMPIC TEAM

Sing to Him a new song; Play skillfully with a shout of joy.
~ Ps. 33:3 (NKJV)

Something that I experienced today, August 10, 2024, at 11:35 AM, thrilled my soul. My husband and I went to the Howard County Athletic Complex to watch our daughter, Cecilia, try out for the Senior Olympic team.

Every woman on the team was over 55 years old. God, many of them had braces on various joints of their body. All of them were excited because they were part of the team trying to qualify for the Olympics.

Father, thank You. I witnessed Your Spirit in them. Your Spirit of pushing forward to reach a goal with like-minded people, striving for the same thing, working beyond their pain or their level of discomfort. I saw You, God, in them. I saw togetherness, calm, love, support, encouragement, and each one helping one another. I saw celebrations when one made a point. I also saw some shouts of joy when one attempted to make the point. It was good to watch them. God, they were working in perfect synergy.

How great it would be if we could act as a team. We, acting as a team, striving to please our heavenly Father and supporting one another, loving each other, helping each other, and moving beyond our level of discomfort to work together as one to reach our heavenly home. There was no division, no attitude, no display of anger that would disrupt the spirit of the team. How great it would be if we could set aside our attitudes and remember our journey, to recall that we want to please our God as we continue in this wilderness.

In Jesus' name, I pray. Amen.

SHARING THE LOAD

Also I heard the voice of the Lord, saying: "Whom shall I send, And who will go for Us?" Then I said, "Here am I! Send me."
~ Isa. 6:8 (NKJV)

Father God, thank You for the Harriet Tubman Cultural Center on Harriet Tubman Lane in Columbia, MD. Today, many festivities are occurring at that site. Today is Harriet Tubman Day. Father, Your children will gather in the name of Jesus. There will be worship, reflections on ancestors and history, shared stories, the breaking of bread, and much happiness. Father, thank You for the opportunity to gather in unity. People from all over will come who are familiar with Howard County. It is another historical moment. There will be catching up with friends, lifting burdens, and lots of hugs and kisses. Many smiles will be shown and received.

There will be some sadness and grief, as there are those who were with the Harriet Tubman Cultural Center in 2023 who are no longer with us in 2024, because some have been called home, while others may be unable to attend the gathering due to illness, catastrophe, or events that have disrupted the flow of life. They will be remembered.

Everybody there will be sharing somebody else's load in some form or fashion. Thank You, God, for the fellowship and the love that will be passing from heart to heart and breast to breast. Thank You for the history. Thank You for the planners and this grand celebration.

In Jesus' name, I pray. Amen.

SUBMIT TO GOD

Therefore submit to God. Resist the devil and he will flee from you. ~ James 4:7 (NKJV)

Father God, in the name of Jesus, I give You praise for another day of thanksgiving. You have been so good to me and my family. We are planning a reunion. It's been a long time since we last saw each other. There are some new members we don't know, and they don't know us either. A reunion seemed to be the major suggestion. The devil constantly rages when the children of God want to honor Him. One of the younger men in the family, now 60 years of age, condemns anyone who would dare to participate in planning or gathering, as it is not real in his mind. According to him, there is no real love, no Christians; we are just playing a game, lying to ourselves. Father, how sad that one person filled with a demonic spirit will not forgive himself for his ungodly actions in past years. Forgive him, Father, he honestly does not know what he is doing. I forgive him. I love him. I carry him in my heart. I pray for him daily. I submit the family to You, Father.

In Jesus' name. Amen.

WAIT ON THE LORD!

But if we hope for what we do not see, we eagerly wait for it with perseverance. ~ Rom. 8:25 (NKJV)

Lord, my heart is heavy, my Spirit low, my soul is vexed, but I know that You are a delivering God! I have history with You. I have known You since my birth; You have known me since before You knitted me in my mother's womb. You know my heart; You know my thoughts from afar. You know my coming and my going. You are aware of my desires and hopes for my children, grandchildren, and great-grandchildren.

There appears to be a lack of morality, and ethics seem to be viewed as a foreign concept. The world appears to applaud ungodly things and shun those that would be pleasing in Your sight. I long for the day when we will honor Your *word*, respect all of life, appreciate the journey, and walk humbly before the ever-present God. Until then, Father, I will wait on You.

In the name of Jesus. Amen.

WALKING BY FAITH, NOT BY SIGHT

So we are always confident, knowing that while we are at home in the body we are absent from the Lord. [7] For we walk by faith, not by sight.
~ 2 Cor. 5:6-7 (NKJV)

Creative, All Seeing, All Viewing, God of the world, You are the One Who allows us to see. Thank You, dear God, for my friend, a 63-year-old black man with severe vision problems. Thank You, Father, for his love of You. Thank You for his faith, trust, and belief in an All-Seeing God who takes care of him abundantly. Father, he works with students at Morgan State University and Coppin State University. He directs and conducts Bible studies with them, and often holds sessions where he discusses how You intervene in the lives of students while they are on campus. He lets them know that while they are struggling with their schoolwork and in their relationships, God is still present. He talks about how faithful You are to them. He is an asset to have on campus. He taught one course at Coppin State and counseled at the Christian Center at Morgan State University. I thank You, for You are his companion; You are the One he holds on to dearly. I prayed to God that he would find a partner with deep faith who cares and loves God as much as he does.

God, I know that You answer prayers. He has found a life partner, one who loves, cares for, and appreciates him for who he is and what he has to offer. Thank You, God, for he has been walking by faith all these years and certainly not by sight. Thank You for his faithfulness and trust in You, and knowing that one day You would send him what he needs in his life. You have done just that, Lord. I thank You, Father, for Your love for my friend. I know You are blessing him as he continues to walk by faith and not by sight. He sets an example for others who may fall in love with Jesus.

It is in His name, I pray. Thank You, Lord, for Faith. Amen.

WALKING WITH GOD

He has shown you, O man, what is good; And what does the Lord require of you But to do justly, To love mercy, And to walk humbly with your God? ~ Mic. 6:8 (NKJV)

God of movement, God of strength, power, and perseverance, I walk with You. I thank You, God, that yesterday at 7:30 PM, my husband asked me if I would like to go for a walk for some exercise. Father, thank You for allowing us to walk together up and down the lane three times yesterday. When I got tired, You sent the rain to cool us off, and then You sent the storm to get us back into the house. I know it was You, God, for You know what we need. I needed that exercise, and You provided it through my husband, who walks every morning with You for 2.5 miles.

I thank You, God, that I was invited to walk with You yesterday. It was a wonderful experience. I began to get tired going up the hill, and You spoke to me, through my husband, by saying, "Take deeper breaths but continue walking." Thank You for the man of God You put in my life, a visionary and a believer who walks with You. I thank You, God, for letting me walk with You.

We follow You in Jesus' name. Amen.

YOUR WORD

For the word of God is alive and active. Sharper than any double-edged sword, it penetrates even to dividing soul and spirit, joints and marrow; it judges the thoughts and attitudes of the heart.
~ Heb. 4:12 (NIV)

Holy Father, the scriptures are nourishment to my soul and a light in my path. It keeps me remembering who I am, who I represent, *who* I belong to, *who* I count on daily, and on *whom* my hope is built. It keeps me on the right path, directs my life, and causes me to tremble when I look at the world and all the upheaval that occurs because of human greed.

Your *word* keeps my tongue cleaved to the roof of my mouth; it keeps me on my knees; it comes to me in the middle of the night; it wakes me in the morning; it calms my grieving soul; I can't live without

Your *word*. Your *word* is the driving force that keeps us clinging to You. Your *word* speaks life to us.

Thank You, in Jesus' name, I pray. Amen.

YOUR WORD MY PURPOSE

Remember your word to your servant, for you have given me hope. My comfort in my suffering is this: Your promise preserves my life.
~ Ps. 119:49-50 (NIV)

Thank You, dear God, for another day of life. Father, sometimes we put things on our agenda that are not important. Things that get in the way of living a wholesome life. Things that delay us from serving You the best that we can. Obstacles that stand in the way of our progress on the Christian journey. The lack of planning by others creates crises in our lives. All are part of the master plan. We need to remember the main thing: Your primary purpose for us. Some people get hung up on, 'Why am I living? Why am I here?'

God, I pray for my understanding of Your purpose for me. I believe, Father, I'm here because You love me and have a plan for me. I'm here because You want me to be impartial and supportive of my sisters and brothers, to have compassion and help the poor, to be gentle in my approach to people, to do as much as I can, for as many as I can, for as long as You give me breath. The obstacles in life will come; they are for my growth. My focus must be clear. My life depends on You. I must live a life that demonstrates my relationship with You, Father. Please, God, strengthen me to live a life worthy of my calling.

In Jesus' name, I pray. Amen.

2 |

FAMILY BONDS

A GODLY MAN FROM YOU

And my God shall supply all your need according to His riches in glory by Christ Jesus. ~ Phil. 4:19 (NKJV)

God, my Father, thank You for providing me with a good husband, a man after Your own heart, a man of Your choosing for me. You have put us together for 52 years. Working side by side for peace and justice for all people. It has not been easy, but that is as it should be, for You have strengthened us for the journey. You gave us good children who worked alongside us, feeding the people without homes on New Year's Eve, New Year's Day, Christmas Day, as well as weekends. You demonstrated that You loved us repeatedly. We have never lacked anything. You always provide for us.

Lord, thank You for Your kindness, love, faith, and presence. All the time, You were leading my husband, and he was leading us. Thank You, Father, for godly men who lead their families to You.

In Jesus' name. Amen.

A PRAYING MOTHER

Confess your trespasses to one another, and pray for one another, that you may be healed. The effective fervent prayer of a righteous man avails much. ~ James 5:16 (NKJV)

God, Mother of the universe, Creator of heaven and earth, Author of our faith, we seek You this day of thanksgiving. Another year has passed, and it is Mother's Day again. Thank You, Father, for another Mother's Day. I remember those whom You put in my life to nurture, guide, and teach me Your precepts.

I carry my mother in my heart. She was a praying woman of faith. She believed that You were her strength and the source of security, love, presence, and abundance in her life. She believed, and because she believed, she taught me to believe. I learned to lean on You, because she leaned on You. Her faith was strong, and she put that faith in me. Thank You, God, for a praying mother. She did as she believed You would have her do. She taught her daughter the ways of the Lord. She taught me to trust and believe in You. Because You are, she is; because she is, I am. The prayers of a righteous mother carried me thus far.

Thank You, in the name of Jesus. Amen.

A SERVANT OF GOD

The Lord will strengthen him on his bed of illness; You will sustain him on his sickbed. ~ Ps. 41:3 (NKJV)

Father, You are a *holy* and *righteous* God of all that is and all that will be. Thank You for last night's slumber, healing, safekeeping, restoration, and abounding love. I praise You for this morning's awakening in my right mind and for giving me the ability to call on You.

One of Your own, a faithful servant in the vineyard, was informed of a lesion on her brain and in her breast. She is depressed and withdrawn.

She has two people whom she helps navigate these waters of life. She is the one they cling to for any help they need. You know all about it, Lord. I know that You are with her. I know You will provide all that she needs to go through this stormy time in her life. Give her strength to go through this valley, knowing that You are with her. Healing and delivering is what You do. She is not alone, Father.

Thank You in the name of Jesus. Amen.

A YOUNGER SISTER'S LOVE

For I through the law died to the law that I might live to God.
~ Gal. 2:19 (NKJV)

Good morning, God! It is 7:45 AM on a cold, rainy, and dark day on August 9, 2024, and we have been under a tornado watch for 24 hours. Father, the night's sleep was very restful. We were resting in Your arms, being taken care of by You, and we had no fear. We know that You are God of the dark as well as God of the light. You are always with us.

The alarm went off on my cell phone for the first time, and I was unfamiliar with that sound. My husband's youngest sister had called our oldest son. There was fear in her heart because the newscaster reported that the tornado was over the township of Lisbon and was heading our way. When she heard his voice, she felt a great sense of relief.

Thank You, God, for the love and concern of a younger sister for her big brother. Again, You provided comfort, assurance, and peace. Thank You for being our Father.

In Jesus' name. Amen.

AT HOME DIALYSIS COUSIN-SISTER

And whatever we ask we receive from Him, because we keep His commandments and do those things that are pleasing in His sight.
~ 1 John 3:22 (NKJV)

O my God, in the name of Jesus, I thank You for my cousin-sister. O God, she was informed by her physician this morning that her kidney function is failing and that she will have to go on dialysis. She wanted home dialysis. God, I know that You are in the plan. I know You, to be a Healer. I know you are a *way Maker* and *mountain mover*. The valley is not too wide nor too deep when You are near.

This situation seems like a mountain to me. O God, she's my cousin-sister. I have known her since her birth. I've taken care of her all her life. I don't remember life before her. Just as I love her, I know You love her more, God, and I know that You know what's best for her.

Strengthen me, dear God, to be here for her. Prepare me to provide answers to any questions or doubts she may have. I'm leaning on You, Lord, this is too big for me. I need You, Lord, we need You, Lord, to handle this situation. I know You can, and I know You will. Healing is what You do, Lord. Spiritually, mentally, or physically, You are the Healer. You have always been there for me. You have always answered my prayers. I have always trusted You, and I know You are not the God of one but the God of all, and I know nothing is too hard for You. Walk with us as we go through this mountain or over it. Bless her husband, son, his wife, and her grandchild, as she shares this information.

With a grateful heart, I thank You, for being my God.

In Jesus' name, I pray. Amen.

BIRTHDAY CELEBRATIONS

And whatever you do in word or deed, do all in the name of the Lord Jesus, giving thanks to God the Father through Him. ~ Col. 3:17 (NKJV)

Father God of all peoples, You have been with us since before our birth. Each year of our life You give us 12 months to do better than the previous year. Thank You, God, for another year, another opportunity to grow in Your service. To be and do more for humankind. You, Father, give us opportunities every year to grow deeper in our faith to witness Your miracles and to share the story of how You brought us through another storm of life. Thank You for allowing us to celebrate with family, friends, and associates.

We could not live one minute without You, Father. It is Your grace and mercy that brings us through. You, Father, are with us every moment of our lives. Thank You for being with us at every birthday celebration. Your presence makes the difference.

In the name of Jesus the Christ. Amen.

BROTHERHOOD

The words of a man's mouth are deep waters; The wellspring of wisdom is a flowing brook. ~ Prov. 18:4 (NKJV)

Father God, thank You for the brotherhood. I give You praise for my husband and his two best friends. You put them together, dear God, when they were 10 years old. They have been best friends, Lord, for 80 years. Thank You, God, for their relationship, and thank You for their support, brother to brother. I honor You, God, for each of them has worked in the vineyard. They are believers in the One True God. They are faithful servants and are examples for others to follow. Thank You, God, for bringing black men together to work in the community, to make a difference in the community and hence in the world. Thank You for their faithfulness, love, and devotion to each other. They are good fathers, husbands, and friends. They are Your disciples, God, they truly follow You. Thank You for being a part of this fellowship. Thank You for their friends and families that support and encourage them. I praise Your name for good men who recognize the brotherhood.

In the name of Jesus the Christ, I pray. Amen.

FATHER, THANK YOU FOR DAUGHTERS

"Fear not, daughter of Zion; Behold, your King is coming, Sitting on a donkey's colt." ~ John 12:15 (NKJV)

Father, thank You for my three daughters. Each one of them has a special relationship with me. Thank You for their tenderness, kindness, and loving concern for me over the years. Thank You for obedient and thoughtful daughters. They have listened, learned, and are supportive of each other. It's so wonderful to see them teaching each other about life. I know, Father, that they have done things that I don't know about. Just as I have done things that my mother didn't know about.

God, thank You for Your grace and mercy, for we have done things that we thought You didn't know about. Sometimes we forget that You are all-knowing and ever-present. Sometimes we forget that You see everything and know everything even before the thoughts form in our mind. You are already aware of what we will do and what we will not do.

Thank You, God, for Your loving kindness and Your forgiving Spirit. You are present with us all the time, everywhere, and every moment of the day. We can never get away from You., just as our daughters can never escape us. You know us quite well. We see each one of our daughters' behavior patterns, their personalities, and how they interact with others. We even know their problem-solving methods.

God, thank You for teaching us how to be parents and for Your Spirit teaching our daughters how to be good daughters. Daughters through the blood of Jesus and by the love of Jesus. Bless each one of my daughters, Father, even when they know or know not what they do.

Thank You, Lord, in the name of Jesus I pray. Amen.

FIFTY-ONE YEARS OF TOGETHERNESS

All that the Father gives Me will come to Me, and the one who comes to Me I will by no means cast out. ~ John 6:37 (NKJV)

Father, I thank You for 51 years with the man whom You prepared me to be his helpmate. Thank You for the opportunity to celebrate these years and the vows that we made to each other and You. They have been good years because You led us through the wilderness of despair, mountains of joy, and the valley of the shadow of death. Through it all, God, You have been right by our side, leading, or putting us back on the right path. You place people of faith, people who believe in You, and people who did not allow us the freedom to think that You were not watching our every move.

Thank You, Father, for our family and Your presence in our lives for 51 years of marriage and 2 years of dating.

In the name of Jesus, I pray. Amen.

FOCUS COMMITTEE

And we know that all things work together for good to those who love
God, to those who are the called according to His purpose.
~ Rom. 8:28 (NKJV)

Father God, thank You for my Focus Committee: Tasha, Cheryl, Doug 3rd, and Cecilia. They are excited about what You are doing in my life, an 81-year-old Black woman, their grandmother, mother, role model, the one who lives in their hearts. Father, I thank You for their wisdom, their patience, and the smiles on their faces as they work with me. They are just precious.

I thank You, God, they know the technology, the various platforms, and all the electronic devices that keep me in quite a quandary. They smile as they remember that they've told me this thing repeatedly, and I still haven't got it. I see their patience. I see them parenting the parent. I am so appreciative. I love to see their smiles. I love seeing how they work together, how they understand each other, and how they support one another, and my heart overflows with joy as I witness it.

Alexandra, God, another one of my granddaughters often helps, but she's now in Graduate School, changing jobs, and doesn't have much time to work with me. I know she is supportive, and often she'll get on and add a statement. I thank You for her contribution.

God, I am so happy, I'm trying to complete this book. The Focus Committee is wonderful, and I love each one of them. They are mine on earth. Thank You, God, for I know we belong to You, and I know that You are in the midst of the plan. None of it could be done without You, dear God, intervening and putting people where they need to be, to work together in harmony. Help us to set an example for others to follow. Thank You, God, for what You're doing in our lives.

In Jesus' name. Amen.

GRANDSONS

Children's children are the crown of old men, And the glory of children is their father. ~ Prov. 17:6 (NKJV)

Thank You, God, for grandsons. Young men in the making. Thank You for their struggles, for the times, God, when they are trying to be older and they're young or trying to be young when they're older. Thank You for the struggles of growing up. Thank You, dear God, for the fears that they may have over moving forward, not knowing what the future might bring, and still being concerned about the present.

Thank You, God, for helping them try to make it and not make mistakes. Oftentimes, Father, they seem to act as if errors are not supposed to be made. Thank You for their perspective regarding failure. Their fears of failing are as if failing is the end of the world. Help them to grow and to know, dear God, that to fall is to get up. To stand where they stood will keep them where they are.

Strengthen them to know, dear God, that with You all things are possible and that the future is not to be feared but revered. We grow from our mistakes, and mistakes are part of life. Thank You, God, for loving, strengthening, and being with us as we navigate life's storms, make mistakes, and face failures. We grow and know that You're always with us.

Thank You for Your presence, in Jesus' name. Amen.

HEALING FOR MY DAUGHTER

Is anyone among you suffering? Let him pray. Is anyone cheerful? Let him sing psalms. ~ James 5:13 (NKJV)

Good afternoon, Father God, our Healer, Savior, and very present Help in the times of storms. I stand in awe of You and all that You do every day for Your children in this world of toil and pain.

Father God, I am asking for healing for my oldest daughter. She has paralysis on the left side of her face. Father, she is Your child. You have called her to preach Your *word*, to be in the service of the Lord, and to serve Your people. She experiences pain when she talks, smiles, and eats. Father, please let the healing balm of Gilead flow throughout her body so that she may find relief and be comforted in knowing that this too shall pass according to Your *will*. Please let it be so.

In Jesus' name, I pray. Amen.

HELP MY NEPHEW, LORD

Likewise the Spirit also helps in our weaknesses. For we do not know what we should pray for as we ought, but the Spirit Himself makes intercession for us with groanings which cannot be uttered.
~ Rom. 8:26 (NKJV)

Father, Healer, Redeemer, and Savior of the world, I come to You this morning, knee bowed and body bent. You are the source of my life.

I bring before You, my nephew. Father, You have been so faithful to him for 39 years. You have blessed his daughter with a kidney transplant. He is a single-parent Father. You have brought them through the surgery. You have kept her focused on her education and her God. You have found favor in the daughter and the father.

You, Lord, made it possible for her to get a 4-year academic scholarship to Duke University. You, Lord, have blessed the father and the daughter with a faith that has not shrunk amid many storms. The father praises You and preaches the gospel of Jesus Christ. The enemy has raised his head and caused the father, my nephew, to weaken. Lord, only You can deliver him from the forces that have come against him.

I trust You, God. Amen.

HONOR THE ELDERS

Let the elders who rule well be counted worthy of double honor, especially those who labor in the word and doctrine. ~ 1 Tim. 5:17 (NKJV)

God, I am so grateful for what You allowed me to witness today. Black men honoring an eighty-nine-year-old Civil Rights Advocate. One who has devoted his life to equality, justice, fair treatment, and freedom for people of color. Father, You made it possible for 75 black men of dignity and wisdom (ages 25-87) to honor Rev. Dr. Douglas Bruce Sands, Sr., for 70 years of active membership in the Alpha Phi Alpha Fraternity. He began his journey at Morgan State University.

Thank You, Father, for leading him in the battle and bringing him through the war. You chose him, Father, to get the honor, but You get the praise.

In Jesus' name. Amen.

LABOR DAY

Let him who stole steal no longer, but rather let him labor, working with his hands what is good, that he may have something to give him who has need. ~ Eph. 4:28 (NKJV)

Father, Jehovah Jireh, thank You for another day. Thank You for the family gatherings. Thank You, dear God, for the love that flows from heart to heart and breast to breast in the immediate family, throughout the neighborhoods, and the cities. I know, God, that love, kindness, joy, and peace are contagious, and we thank You that as we move about and see people, we can spread love, joy, and peace.

Our family gathered today, celebrating the end of the Summer season and the beginning of the Fall season. We gathered outside. It was a lovely day. The kids were playing, while family members talked and greeted one another. The food was being placed on the tables. As I looked at my family and the children who gathered, my heart swelled with joy. I knew, dear God, that You were in our midst. I felt Your presence. I knew that the Spirit of the Lord was in this place. I felt the blessings of the Lord all around us. As I walked among my family, I heard people praising You. Some discussed the nation's politics and the impact that our decisions will have on other countries. I lifted my hands to the heavens and said, 'God, Your *will* be done in all our lives and every nation and every person wherever they are right now, in the name of Jesus.'

I trust You, Father. I honor and I love You. Thank You for my family being here. Thank You for the joy that each person feels.

In the name of Jesus, I pray. Amen.

LOVE ONE ANOTHER

We love Him because He first loved us. ~ 1 John 4:19 (NKJV)

Loving, *holy, righteous* God of the universe, fill me with overflowing, outpouring love. Thank You, God, for loving me unconditionally. Regardless of what I do or where I go, Your love still abounds. Whatever or whoever I see, whatever I say, whatever I hear, Your love is still with me. Regardless of how others perceive me or how I perceive myself, Your love is still with me. Irrespective of whether I feel good or bad, whether I'm sick or well, Your love still surrounds me. Regardless of my thoughts, which may be godly or ungodly, You still love me.

Father, pour into me and others the same love that You have for us. Let us love one another as You love us. Please remove complaints, ill wishes, or any negativity that may interfere with the flow of love between one person and another. Let us love, O God, like we've never loved before. Our lives depend on it. Love is the very foundation of our life. It is all in You, it begins in You, it ends in You. It is You.

Thank You, Lord. In Jesus' name, I pray. Amen.

REUNIONS

To all who are in Rome, beloved of God, called to be saints: Grace to you and peace from God our Father and the Lord Jesus Christ.
~ Rom. 1:7 (NKJV)

Thank You, Father God, for allowing Your children in every school of life to gather and celebrate Your blessings. All their experiences were stepping-stones, which You provide, for growth and development. Thank You, Father, for paving their way through high school, college, and post-graduate work. Thank You, God, for guiding their steps through trade schools, on-the-job training opportunities, and general work experiences.

Thank You for giving men, women, and children the opportunity to render love, faith, generosity, and service to others. Thank You for the chance to see each other one more time. Thank You for those who have already gone to their new home in glory. Thank You for those who are ill, still trusting in Your grace. Thank You for those who are actively transitioning. Thank You for those who are living life very prosperously. Thank You for those who are struggling. Thank You for those who are in and of the world. Thank You for the faint-hearted. Thank You for Your witnesses.

Thank You, Father God. You allowed us to gather, to show love, patience, faithfulness, tenderness, kindness, and to realize that it is a level field with You. We are all Yours. You are with us right here, right now. Thank You, Father, for this reunion.

In Jesus' name. Amen.

SEVEN-YEAR-OLD CHILDREN WANT TO PLAY

The nursing child shall play by the cobra's hole, And the weaned child shall put his hand in the viper's den. ⁹ They shall not hurt nor destroy in all My holy mountain, For the earth shall be full of the knowledge of the Lord As the waters cover the sea. ~ Isa. 11:8-9 (NKJV)

Father God, it's playtime at seven years of age. It's a time of learning how to navigate through the summer and the winter. The summer is spent playing with other kids and doing things like learning to swim, playing ball, and just having good, clean fun. It's the time when they're out of the 1st grade. They know they're going to the second grade, and life is getting more serious in their parents' eyes.

Father, You know little children want to play and have fun. Bless them all as they're having fun, enjoying life, and have limited responsibilities. Time flies quickly, Father. The time will come shortly when the children begin to take on some responsibilities, and the parents will have higher expectations of them. It's called the learning process.

School pictures must be taken. The young boys' hair must be cut, and the young girls' hair conditioned, braided, and ready to start school. These things take time from their busy play schedule. Out of frustration, they cry because they don't know anything else to do. Their parents, like You, Father, know what's best for them as You know what's best for us, and so they continue their plan for school.

Thank You, God, for times of preparation. Thank You for the time to play. Thank You, God, for times of remembering yesteryear. Thank You, God, for the time when we were children, we could play and not worry about the cares of the world. Thank You for innocent little children who just want to play.

In Jesus' name. Amen.

SISTER FRIEND

Let nothing be done through selfish ambition or conceit, but in lowliness of mind let each esteem others better than himself.
~ Phil. 2:3 (NKJV)

God, my father, You are my present Help in every kind of trouble. Keep me under Your watchful eye, Father. Heighten Your Spirit of discernment in me. Keep me truthful all the time. Guide my tongue so that I may not say anything that will hurt or cause anyone to stumble on this journey in the maze of life. When my sisters are being vicious and trying to bring another sister down, strengthen me to be a calming influence and bring truth, love, comfort, and Your *word* of life, reminding them that we should look after the best interests of each other, not just our own. Help me to be a good representative of You, to remind them of who we are and *whose* we are, and to remind them of our joy in pleasing You as sisters and friends.

In Jesus' name. Amen.

SISTERHOOD SOLIDARITY

Therefore be patient, brethren, until the coming of the Lord.
See how the farmer waits for the precious fruit of the earth, waiting patiently for it until it receives the early and latter rain. You also be patient.
Establish your hearts, for the coming of the Lord is at hand.
~ James 5:7-8 (NKJV)

Father, I thank You for the 16 senior sisters who are in the struggle to help our younger sisters realize that they have a purpose. Thank You for

Dr. Salema Marriott, who always wants to include everyone. Her voice has constantly challenged other women to speak out, to go the extra mile, and to walk in another sister's shoes. She has always been one to speak for the disenfranchised, the imprisoned, the voiceless, the lonely, homeless, and fearful women whose faith may not be strong. These 16 women trust You, Lord, for we know You hear our cries and pity every groan. Thank You for Your strength. Thank You for Your presence when we face trials while on our journey.

In Jesus' name. Amen.

THE LOVE OF CHILDREN

Behold, children are a heritage from the Lord, The fruit of the womb is a reward. ~ Ps. 127:3 (NKJV)

Creative and *holy righteous* God, I give You praise for the love of my children. Father, thank You for their devotion and care for us.

We were having difficulty completing our taxes. One daughter called to say she's on her way and she will take care of the taxes today. Thank You, Father. That was an issue that was pressing heavily on my mind. It needed to be completed before October 1. Although it was necessary, I was not ready to initiate the process or seek assistance. Thankfully, I did not have to call for help. Our daughter, the Accountant, came and completed the taxes for 2023. Thank You, God, for her sensitivity to our needs. The taxes are filed and the penalty is known.

Father, I know that You will make a way because that's who You are. Thank You for the love of our daughter. Thank You for the love of our children. Thank You for her sensitive care, understanding, and patience with us. They are Yours, and they exemplify You quite well. Thank You, Father, in the name of Jesus, for our youngest daughter. You have blessed her with excellent skills.

In Jesus' name, we pray. Amen.

THREE LITTLE BOYS, THREE GROWN MEN

Behold, children are a heritage from the Lord, The fruit of the womb is a reward. ~ Ps. 127:3 (KJV)

Father, thank You for my three little grandsons. I remember their little stories, their playing together for two weeks every summer for 11 Years, at the "big house" in Mt. Airy. They called the parsonage in Annapolis, our "little house." They loved each other and constantly tried to outdo one another. They loved the outside. They would play games such as Hide and Seek, Tag, throwing the stick the longest distance, telling the most interesting story, as well as running for your life, among many others. They had the most fun, taking care of Granddad while I was at the office.

They slept on the family room floor in their sleeping bags. They would watch TV, laugh, giggle, and eat snacks all night. They would fall asleep in front of the TV every night after 1 AM, never using their beds. They did not want to be away from each other. That is the way it is, Lord. Your Spirit binds them together. They wanted it to last a little longer. They knew that soon the time would be over, and they would be separated until next year.

Each one had quiet time with each of their grandparents. Each one prayed, first thing in the morning and the last thing at night, with their grandparents before the grandparents retired for the evening. The boys read the Bible each morning before breakfast. They would share their interpretation of the scripture with their grandmother.

Father, thank You for the love, joy, unity, peace, and innocence of three little boys. They knew You then and know You now for themselves. Thank You, God, for the experience of teaching, loving, and watching them grow into three wonderful, strong, faithful young men who understand the bonds, unity, and faithfulness of knowing and trusting in You, knowing that through You all things are possible.

In Jesus' name, I pray. Amen.

THREE OF YOUR CHILDREN

And Peter said unto him, Aeneas, Jesus Christ maketh thee whole: arise, and make thy bed. And he arose immediately. ~ *Acts 9:34 (KJV)*

Good morning, Father. Thank You for another day. All night long, as we slept, You were with us. You strengthened us, spoke to us, and prepared us for this day. I place my children before You today. Three of them have health challenges.

My oldest daughter has paralysis of a nerve on the left side of her face. My daughter, Robin, is battling stage 4 cancer. Bless each branch of the family. My youngest son, Curtis, is battling with addiction, HIV, Hep B, and has just been diagnosed with Hep C.

Bless each of them with Your healing, Father, I pray. Let Your healing be spiritual, mental, psychological, physical, social, economic, political, or whatever is in Your *will*; only You can heal completely.

I thank You, Father. In Jesus' name. Amen.

3

GOD IN THE MIDST

BREATH OF GOD

*Nor is He worshiped with men's hands, as though He needed any-
thing, since He gives to all life, breath, and all things.*
~ Acts 17:25 (NKJV)

Eternal God, I come to You today in intercessory prayer for my little
sister. Father, she is having difficulty breathing. I plead the blood of Jesus over her lungs and her entire respiratory system. I know, God, that
You know what's best for her. I know that You know her situation far
better than I do. I know that she belongs to You.

I come to You, God, asking for healing for her. If her lungs are mal-
functioning, God, please restore them and have her lungs function according to Your divine *will* and way. Allow her, Father, to slow down
just a little bit and recognize that she is not alone. You are always with
her 24/7, 365 days a year. I declare and decree that no weapon drawn
against her or anything coming from an ungodly source will prosper in
her life. You are her *healer, deliverer,* Savior, and her Lord. Thank You,
God, for making her whole and giving her air to breathe.

In Jesus' name, I pray. Amen.

CHANGE OF SEASONS

To everything there is a season, A time for every purpose under heaven:
~Eccles. 3:1 (NKJV)

Thank You, Father, as summer ends, a new season is about to begin. Thank You, Father, for September. Thank You for the fall season. Thank You, God, no increase in the heating or air conditioning bill this month. We get a small break. Thank You, God, for Your rich provisions.

Father, I see the change of season. I see the leaves falling in the yard; they are a mix of yellow, green, and brown. It's beginning to look so pretty; it looks like fall. Thank You, I love this season. There's a briskness in the air, a fresh breeze, the sun shines brightly, and yet it's nice and cool.

Thank You, God, for just as You change the seasons in nature, You change the seasons of our lives. There are seasons when things are rough, and then there are seasons when we get a break; it seems like everything is leveling out. I give You praise, God, for You show us our lives as we look at nature and the creation that surrounds us.

In the name of Jesus. Amen.

CHRISTMAS SEASON

This is My commandment, that you love one another as I have loved
you. ~ John 15:12 (NKJV)

God of this wonderful season of love, hope, joy, peace, and gentleness, You sent Your Son as a newborn baby into this world of deceit, trouble, pain, distrust, conditional love, and toil. You knew what Your children needed. Everybody loves a newborn baby. A baby so helpless, one who cannot do anything to help himself but depends on those around him to provide his every need. You sent Your Son to show us how to live, support, love, provide for, and be present for one another, and to encourage us to be our brother's keeper. Thank You for this wonderful gift.

In Jesus' name. Amen.

CLING TO GOD

For as the sash clings to the waist of a man, so I have caused the whole house of Israel and the whole house of Judah to cling to Me,' says the Lord, 'that they may become My people, for renown, for praise, and for glory; but they would not hear.' ~ Jer. 13:11 (NKJV)

God, of Grace and Glory on all Your people, pour out Your restorative power, this Monday morning. I pray for strength for Your people, to cling to Your *word* of life, and to live in constant hope of life eternal.

Thank You for holding me close to You. Thank You for allowing Your Spirit to teach me to cling to You and making it real that You are my Source of life. Without You, there is no joy, no peace, and no hope.

Thank You for wanting only the best for me. I am Your child, Your servant. I give You all the praise and all the glory. Please speak to me, Father. I am listening.

In Jesus' name. Amen.

FAWNS BEING OBEDIENT

Then God said, "Let there be light"; and there was light. And God saw the light, that it was good; and God divided the light from the darkness. ~ Gen. 1:3-4 (NKJV)

Father God, in the name of Jesus, thank You for this afternoon. The rain is falling very hard. I hear it falling on the window in the ceiling. I look out and see two fawns standing at the edge of the forest as if they were wondering - what is going on. My soul is content as I'm in my home, and I think about the goodness of God and how great You have been to us. I rejoice in my spirit, and I cry out, "Hallelujah, thank You, God, for the day." As I continue looking out the window, Lord, at Your creation, I see the fawns standing in amazement. I watched their mother or their father watching, and I believe that they were looking at me. I see, I know, I feel there is some communication between the parents and the babies, as they wander close to them and stand side by side.

That's the way it is with You, Father. When You see us standing in amazement and about to do something wrong, You speak to our inner core, calling us back to You. Sometimes we act like a fawn and run back to You, we step away from the danger because You have called us back.

Father, it would be lovely if we would never forget, as we look at nature, that You call us back to You day after day, just like the mother deer calls her fawns. They came to her. Remind us to be obedient and to always run to You.

In Jesus' name, we pray. Amen.

GIFTS OF LOVE

Be kindly affectionate to one another with brotherly love, in honor giving preference to one another; not lagging in diligence, fervent in spirit, serving the Lord; ~ Rom. 12:10-11 (NKJV)

Father, thank You for making it possible for me to mail some packages that are gifts of love to family members in North Carolina, New Orleans, Georgia, and Texas. I have been trying to send these packages for a little over a week. The opportunity presented itself for the mailing to occur today. Thank You, God, for You were in the plan all along.

Thank You for my husband's ability to drive and for him being such a safe driver. He takes me on errands without even giving it a thought. Thank You for his willingness, as he realizes that I cannot drive due to my impaired vision.

Father, You were with me as I mailed the packages, as I received a good report from my cardiologist, and as we rolled along, You kept us safe from hurt, harm, and danger. Father, You allowed us to walk two miles in the mall today. It's been a mighty good day, God. Thank You for allowing us the time to mail these gifts of love to our family.

In Jesus' name, I pray. Amen.

GOD WILL SHOW UP

And my God shall supply all your need according to His riches in glory by Christ Jesus. ~ Phil. 4:19 (NKJV)

God, our Father, Healer, Deliverer, Provider, Savior, and Lord of lords. Thank You for always showing up right on time. Whenever there is an issue, You show up. When I am low in spirit, when I am not feeling well, when I am doubtful, when I am laden over one of my children, You show up. When I am concerned about my employment, when I feel that things could be better, when there is a financial crunch, or when one of my family members is ill, You show up. When I'm uneasy about relationships, when I need to let go, or when I have received news about one of my friends having problems, You show up. When there is a crisis in the city, when there is discomfort in the community, God, You always show up! When You show up, You show out. Everything is wonderful when You show up.

Thank You, God, in the name of Jesus. Amen.

GOD'S TEAM

And we know that all things work together for good to those who love God, to those who are the called according to His purpose.
~ Rom. 8:28 (NKJV)

Thank You for being who You are to the world. Thank You for having me on Your team. My delight is serving You.

There is nothing like knowing that you have a Savior, a Provider, a Friend, and a Guiding Light. You are our Captain. We do as You instruct. Often, we miss the mark. We ask for forgiveness for all our near misses and almost-made-it. Thank You for always calling the plays for us to make. Strengthen us to be good team members, to be supportive of one another, and always to encourage others. Thank You, God.

In the name of Jesus. Amen.

I NEED MORE...

And my God shall supply all your need according to His riches in glory by Christ Jesus. ~ *Phil. 4:19 (NKJV)*

Lord of the weary, the downtrodden, the hardheaded, the slovenly, the nay-sayer, the hard-hearted, the constant complainer, the know-it-all, You are the Lord of those who always need more; the people who never have enough. Even when they have an abundance, it is never enough; they need more!

You, O Lord, who loves and provides for us, open our minds so that we may recognize that we need to share our blessings with others, not try to save our blessings from others. Remind us, O Lord, that all of us belong to You. You show no partiality. You love unconditionally, You provide equally, and we are Yours. We lack nothing because we have You. You are all that we need.

In Jesus' name. Amen.

LOSING A FRIEND

A friend loves at all times, And a brother is born for adversity. ~ *Prov. 17:17 (NKJV)*

God, my Father, thank You for this day. Thank You for the opportunity to pray to a known God who is all-powerful and is ever-present with us. Thank You, Father, for the joy of having friends and family nearby. Thank You for the love that flows from heart to heart and breast to breast between those who live in a specific location. Thank You, God, that we can move wherever we choose to and set down roots to live in peace. Thank You for the people we meet along our journey, people whom we may encounter in new locations. Thank You that we can, with God's help, build relationships and find comfort in people who have relocated, and we find ourselves in a strange place. Thank You that we're able to reach out to one another and know that we belong to the highest, God. I give You praise for the friends we have met along the journey, for the long-standing relationships that are faithful and true.

Today, dear God, I pray for a friend of my little sister. She is moving to North Carolina. They both are sad. They moved to this location 20 years ago and have formed a relationship; now it's time to separate. Both are grieving, Father. I ask in the name of Jesus that You strengthen them as they move about, so they may build new relationships. Allow each of them to continue remembering one another, to stay in contact, to pray for each other, and to recall that they are all a family traveling together. Let them not forget that one day they will see each other when they get home with the Father. Thank You for the opportunity, God.

In Jesus' name. Amen.

NEIGHBORHOOD TERRORS

Therefore I remind you to stir up the gift of God which is in you through the laying on of my hands. ⁷ For God has not given us a spirit of fear, but of power and of love and of a sound mind.
~ 2 Tim. 1:6-7 (NKJV)

Lord God, in the name of Jesus, I come to You for peace and safety. There is a senior neighborhood in Florida that has been terrorized by persons unknown. We know it is the work of the ungodly spirit. One lady's house was broken into last night, and she was shot in the head. It is a Senior development, God, and all the people are worried sick. I plead the blood of Jesus over the community. I plead the blood of Jesus over the people in the community and their homes. I declare and decree right now in the name of Jesus that no person or thing aimed at the destruction of God's children will be successful. I plead the blood for safety, healing, restoration, peace of mind, sense of joy, and an increased faith in the one who can save them. They are not alone. There is One who protects them and is constantly with them.

Thank You, God, for Your saving grace not only for that neighborhood in Florida but for every neighborhood. I give You praise for covering them with Your grace and mercy, thank You in advance.

In the name of Jesus. Amen.

NINETY YEARS WITH GOD

The days of our lives are seventy years; And if by reason of strength they are eighty years, Yet their boast is only labor and sorrow; For it is soon cut off, and we fly away. ~ Ps. 90:10 (NKJV)

Lord, thank You for my husband's 90 years in this wilderness—90 years of being under Your mighty hand. You have led him through some mighty dangerous paths in the '60s and the '70s. Many efforts have been made in the hope of achieving equality and justice for Indigenous people worldwide. Many people joined organized Marches, protest movements, and boycotts to survive in a society that is divided by color.

Thank You, God, for protecting, guiding, comforting, and always being there for this man of God. Thank You, Lord, for doing all that You do for this man of God.

All in the name of Jesus. Amen.

NO DIVIDING LINES BETWEEN US

Now I urge you, brethren, note those who cause divisions and offenses,
contrary to the doctrine which you learned, and avoid them.
~Rom. 16:17 (NKJV)

Today is a day of Thanksgiving. You are doing a new thing in our nation. Thank You for using women to bring about unity, peace, justice, and equality for all. Madam Kamala Harris, Vice President of the United States, is the democratic nominee for President of the United States. Women around the globe are watching and waiting with bated breath. In the United States, women are gathering in groups, volunteering and working together to bring about a change in this country. We are working to be supportive in any way possible for Madam Kamala Harris, the Presidential Nominee.

Our work for the sisterhood is real. There are no dividing lines between us, God. I believe that is Your *will*. I believe You want us to stand up for equality. I further believe You want us to listen and obey Your *will* and Your *way*. The only way we can do that, God, is to stand up and do what is right in every situation We need to work together, pray together, and unite in our efforts to support the democratic Presidential Nominee, and to pray for her as she listens to Your still, quiet voice and remember that You are God of the universe. We belong to You, and You want us just to do what is always right and to remember that Your *word* is nourishment for our spirit and our souls. Listening to You, Father God, following You can only bring peace, unity, justice, and equality for all in our nation.

Thank You, God, for being in Madam Harris. Thank You, God, for no dividing line between us.

In Jesus' name, I pray. Amen.

OUR OVERCOMING FATHER

He who overcomes, I will make him a pillar in the temple of My God, and he shall go out no more. I will write on him the name of My God and the name of the city of My God, the New Jerusalem, which comes down out of heaven from My God. And I will write on him My new name. ~ Rev. 3:12 (NKJV)

Our Father, help me to hold fast to my faith in You. Give me strength and courage not to give up under pressure. When I seem to lose my way, Lord, You find me and put me back on course. Thank You for walking in front of me, to keep Satan from destroying me. Thank You for always protecting me from the evils of this world. Father, You know my thoughts from afar. My coming and going are well known to You. In my weakest moment, Your presence is felt. My strength comes from You, Lord. You are the *overcomer*. Because You are, I too am an overcomer.

In Jesus' name, I pray. Amen.

PARENTING IS A WONDERFUL GIFT

but glory, honor, and peace to everyone who works what is good, to the Jew first and also to the Greek. [11] For there is no partiality with God. ~ Rom. 2:10-11 (NKJV)

Father, thank You for being such a great parent. Thank You for teaching us how to be parents. Thank You, God, for reminding us that we were once children, teenagers, young adults, and finally adults. Thank You for the joy of remembering our childhood and the smiles that come to our faces when we recall the little things we did as we navigated through life's waters. Thank You, God, we reflect on our children and the little things they did as they navigated through life's waters. Just as we oftentimes get frustrated and shake our heads over whether our children will ever get it. I know that our parents did the same thing.

There had to be times when they wrung their hands and shook their heads and thought, "Will my child ever grow up?" Father, I know that there are times when You shake Your head and turn to the heavenly beings and say, "Will they ever get it?"

I've learned throughout the years that I can trust in Jesus. I know my parents trusted in Jesus, and I've learned, Father, that through it all, the children need our help. Oftentimes, we may get it right, but we try so hard because we love them. Father, You love us so well. You'll never leave us, never forsake us, never turn Your back on us, and You'll never give up on us. Just as You never let us go, we learn to hold on to our children and never let them go because of the love that flows from You to us. The love that flowed down all these generations is the same love that flows to us and our children, and our children's children. It's a wonderful gift to think about how You love us and how You parent us every day.

Thank You, Lord, in the name of Jesus I pray. Amen.

SATAN, YOU CANNOT WIN

So He called them to Himself and said to them in parables: "How can Satan cast out Satan? ~ Mark 3:23 (NKJV)

Thank You, Father, for waking me up this morning. Father, You kept us all during the night. I know all power is in Your hands. I know You are the Savior. With You, nothing is impossible. Deliverance is in Your hands. What I cannot see, what I cannot be, what I cannot do, what I cannot solve, all belong to You! You are the problem solver. You can do everything. You are our all and all.

I am not willing to lose my son, Curtis Owen Sands, to Satan. I demand, in the name of Jesus, "Satan, remove your hands from my son, remove your evil thoughts from his mind. Set him free; he belongs to God. He is not yours."

There is nothing that God cannot do. What God cannot do does not exist. In the name of Jesus, release him and let him go. I come before you, Satan, as a child of the living King of kings and Lord of lords. The One who owns all, even you. He allows you to exist. You have no power!" Thank You, God, for being who You are! I love and honor You.

In the name of Jesus. Amen.

SCHOOL SHOOTING IN GEORGIA

Therefore submit to God. Resist the devil and he will flee from you.
~James 4:7 (NKJV)

Father God, in the name of Jesus, I bring before You today the school in Georgia, where there was a shooting this morning. Father, we ask in the name of Jesus that You bless the principal, the teachers, all the students, and all the school personnel. Thank You, dear God, for putting Your arms of protection around the community in which the school is located. Thank You, God, for we just discovered that the news media and the police are all over the school looking for the shooter, but giving an account of what has occurred to the public.

Satan has raised his head again on the very first day of school. We heard that two adults and two children were killed, and 30 people were hurt. God, that's too much human carnage going on right now in this universe. I plead the blood of Jesus over all schools, all students, all teachers, and over all gatherings. I decree and declare right now that Satan does not have any control over this world. He has no control over the students, the government, the economy, or anything else. He is just raising his head, trying to destroy God's people.

In the name of Jesus, I plead the blood, Father God, over everybody. I ask, God, in the name of Jesus, that Satan be removed, isolated, so that he can no longer harm Your children. We belong to You. We know we are Yours whether sitting up or lying down.

Father, cast Satan into the gates of hell, I pray. Thank You, God, for the peace that I feel right now knowing that much is being done for these children who have been attacked viciously. The police, dear God, the hospitals, doctors, and nurses, the nation is in prayer, waiting, and trying to do all they can to bring about some peace and harmony. Only You, God, can make this nation whole. This is Your world, and I am so thankful that You are in charge. Have Your way with all of us, God, have Your way.

In Jesus' name, I pray. Amen.

STRANDED WITH JESUS

The Lord is near to all who call upon Him, To all who call upon Him in truth. ~ Ps. 145:18 (NKJV)

God of all, to You we pray, for people stranded on the highway. Please bless this family, LORD. I know You will, I know You can; this is what You do. Father, it looks like they are parked, but the police are there with them. I do not know what the situation is, Father. I know You to be a Savior, a Provider, and a very Present Help in times of trouble. They may be stranded, but are not alone. Jesus is there with them. Thank You for Your Son. I know He is interceding on their behalf.

In His name, I pray. Amen.

STRENGTHEN ME, FATHER

In the day when I cried out, You answered me, And made me bold with strength in my soul. ~ Ps. 138:3 (NKJV)

Father, I cry out to You this morning. My soul is fearful. I have been asked to mediate a family crisis. I do not want anyone to be hurt. Lord, I need You to guide and strengthen me to speak truth to power. Your power, love, gentleness, kindness, compassion, grace, and mercy. As I cry out to You this morning, I know that You will strengthen me.

Thank You, Father, in the name of Jesus. Amen.

THE ARCH OF SAFETY

I will not leave you orphans; I will come to you. ~ John 14:18 (NKJV)

Creative God, thank You for keeping my son under the arch of safety. Father, thank You for bringing him back from overdosing four times, of which I am aware. Thank You for being with us every moment of our lives. Thank You for having Your Son, Jesus, die on the cross for every soul. You tell us that every soul belongs to You, Father. I believe You, I trust You, and I know You for myself. I have history with You. There are no limits to what You can do.

I thank You, God, with every fiber of my body. Thank You for keeping my son. I know You love him. Thank You for keeping Your hands on him and never letting him go. You are living in him, Father. He belongs to You. I love him. He is Yours, Father God. May Your *will* be manifested in his head and heart.

Thank You, Father, for one more day under the arch of safety.

In Jesus' name. Amen.

THE CLOSE OF THE DAY

Let us therefore come boldly to the throne of grace, that we may obtain mercy and find grace to help in time of need. ~ Heb. 4:16 (NKJV)

The day is ending, Father, shadows of the evening are falling across the sky. Thank You, God, for the opportunity to talk to You tonight. Thank You for all that You've done and the blessings You've rendered upon all Your children by the blood of Jesus, or by the blood of man, through the love of Jesus, or the love of man. Your love sustains all of us. Your love binds us together and keeps us doing what we should. Oftentimes it may seem hard, but You, O Lord, keep us remembering Whose we are, and who we are, as well as Who we serve. We serve You, O Lord, from sunup until sundown. Let it be so, Lord, please let it be so.

Forgive us for our transgressions and iniquities. Try us again tomorrow morning, if it is Your *will*. We will be ever so grateful to give You the honor and the praise. Even in our subconsciousness, speak to us and tell us what You desire us to do on the morrow, Lord. Strengthen our minds to be obedient to You, Lord.

In the name of Jesus, I pray. Amen.

THE GRACE OF GOD

And He said to me, "My grace is sufficient for you, for My strength is made perfect in weakness." Therefore most gladly I will rather boast in my infirmities, that the power of Christ may rest upon me.
~ 2 Cor. 12:9 (NKJV)

Creative, Holy, Righteous, and Good God of the universe, thank You for Your grace and Your tender mercies. Father, Your grace woke me this morning in my right mind. It was Your Grace that made it possible for me to get up and put my feet on the floor without falling or stumbling. It was Your Grace that allowed me to brush my teeth or take a sip of water without strangling. Your grace, God, allowed me to see the bright sunshine and to walk about the house. Your grace, God, allowed me to shower without falling and hurting myself. Your grace, God, allowed me to sit down in a chair and to be able to eat a meal and not get strangled. God, truly it is Your grace and mercy that surrounds me, that keeps us upright and moving. It is Your grace that keeps my mind working so that I can know and remember that without You, I am nothing. In the powerful and mighty name of Jesus, *who* is the Christ,

I thank Your God this morning for Your grace. Amen.

THE UNGODLY SPIRIT OF CONTROL

Draw near to God and He will draw near to you. Cleanse your hands,
you sinners; and purify your hearts, you double-minded.
~ James 4:8 (NKJV)

Father God, this is a beautiful day for Your children to live, laugh, work, play, and be at peace with one another. Dear God, I ask You in the name of Jesus to remove the ungodly spirit of control that seems to be looming large among Your people today. That ungodly spirit of control, dear God, blocks, separates, and keeps others from being all that they can be. That ungodly spirit of control, dear God, isolates and separates people who should be on one accord. That ungodly spirit of control wants to expand. That ungodly spirit of control wants to decide who, what, when, where, and how. That ungodly spirit stifles Your people, God, and keeps them from being the very best that they can be. It also prevents others within the range of that ungodly spirit from fulfilling their needs. Father, I ask You, in the name of Jesus, to cast the ungodly spirit out of Your people. Strengthen us to be who You want us to be and not who the ungodly spirit of control wants us to be. I thank You, Father. I know You'll see us through.

In Jesus' name, I pray. Amen.

THE UNGODLY SPIRIT OF DECEIT

Be of the same mind toward one another. Do not set your mind on
high things, but associate with the humble. Do not be wise in your own
opinion. Repay no one evil for evil. Have regard for good things in the
sight of all men. ~ Rom. 12:16-17 (NKJV)

Thank You, God, for my sisters and brothers. Thank You for providing me with such a large family. I praise Your name for loving us.

Father, forgive us for our waywardness. Forgive us for the things that we do that are simply not pleasing in Your sight. Sometimes, Father, one of Your children may intentionally try to deceive another, for purposes unknown. Forgive us for that ungodly spirit of deceit that oftentimes enters us and causes us to say and do things that we know are not right. Father, we know that intentionally deceiving and misleading another is wrong. We know that it grieves Your Spirit. It hurts and causes harm to the person who is being deceived, and it causes equal harm and pain to the one who has embraced the ungodly spirit of deceit.

Father, I ask in the name of Jesus that this ungodly spirit of deceit be removed from the face of the earth. We don't need it. We shouldn't use it. We can't embrace it and expect to please You, Father. Our lives are to be lived in such a way that it's not only pleasing to You, but also pleasing to those who are watching us. Our lives need to be pleasing to those who will follow us, O God. In the name of Jesus, Father, make us strong that we can refuse all ungodly spirits. I thank You, God, for hearing my prayer. I know You'll come through.

In Jesus' name I pray. Amen.

THE UNGODLY SPIRIT OF LYING

I hate and abhor lying, But I love Your law. ~ Ps. 119:163 (NKJV)

Divine Redeemer, Great God of Peace, thank You for the morning bright. Thank You for family and friends around the globe. Thank You for lifting my head this morning. Thank You for the movement of my limbs. Praise You for all that You will do to bless my family and everybody in the universe.

Father, I declare and decree that the ungodly spirit of lying that has entered Your children be removed. The ungodly spirit of lying is causing too much divisiveness, too many distractions, too many disruptions, and too much disturbance in our souls today. I pray that truth may be spoken to power. Please let truth reign in the world. Truth can stand alone. Father, I declare and decree that the ungodly spirit of lying be removed, in the name of Jesus. Thank You, Father, for Your grace and Your mercy.

In the name of Jesus, I pray. Amen.

TRAVELING IN FAITH

who through Him believe in God, who raised Him from the dead and gave Him glory, so that your faith and hope are in God.
~ 1 Pet. 1:21 (NKJV)

Almighty Father, Savior of Heaven and Earth, You are the Master Provider of everything that dwells below the sky. I see a family in need of help right now. Their mode of transportation appears to be on its last legs. The windows are all broken, and the tires appear to be flat. The car seems to have been in an accident. It has bent fenders, peeling paint, and side mirrors that appear to be on the verge of falling. The tags indicate they are from Pennsylvania. They are traveling on faith.

Father, in the name of Jesus, please help them to reach their destination and return home. Thank You, Father.

In the name of Jesus. Amen.

TRAVELING MERCIES

I cried out to You, O Lord: I said, "You are my refuge, My portion in the land of the living. ~ Ps. 142:5 (NKJV)

Father, thank You for being with my daughter, who traveled from Virginia today. Thank You for my children, husband, grandchildren, great-grandchildren, all my immediate relatives, and cousins around the world. It is a great day because we serve a God who has all power, strength, wisdom, and has never lost a battle. Thank You, Father, for being a Burden Bearer for Your children. Thank You for taking care of all of us as we travel to and fro.

In the name of Jesus. Amen.

WHY WORRY

"So do not start worrying: 'Where will my food come from? or my drink? or my clothes?' ~ Matt. 6: 31 (GNT)*

God, our constant Friend, Savior, and Father, in times like these, we realize just how much we depend on Your grace and mercy to sustain us. The number of people without homes is increasing, unemployment is high, and people are reluctant to return to offices to work. The government is on the verge of shutting down, and the cost of food is rising.

I am assured there's no need to worry, because You're in control of everything. God, in Your time, You will make it right. I do not worry!

In the name of Jesus. Amen.

Y & C CONSIGNMENT SHOP

What has happened before will happen again. What has been done before will be done again. There is nothing new in the whole world. ~ Eccles. 1:9 (GNT)*

Father God, in the name of Jesus, I thank You for new adventures. Thank You for the opportunities to accept new challenges. Thank You for the opportunity to relocate, find employment, and start a business. Thank You, dear God, for my daughter, Cecilia, who now resides in Virginia Beach. She is making new friends and getting a new lease on life. She's excited about the new adventure she is embarking on with Yvette. They are starting a consignment shop. God, thank You for their courage to step out on faith. Thank You for their friendship and thank You, dear God, for family. I know You will continue to bless them in their adventure, bless them in their work, and bless them on their spiritual journey. Thank You for leading them where You want them to go. God, please keep them safe from both external and internal forces. May each of them remember that You are the God of their salvation and that without You, there is no other. Thank You, Father, I love You.

In the name of Jesus. Amen.

4

REVERENCE & PRAISE

101 DEGREES TODAY

Trust in Him at all times, you people; Pour out your heart before Him; God is a refuge for us. Selah ~ Ps. 62:8 (NKJV)

Upon awakening this morning, I saw the bright sunshine peeking through the window. I give praise to You, Father, for being able to see one more day. As I said my prayers, I felt the heat in the house. I realized it was going to be a mighty hot day. God, Your goodness has been rendered upon the people of this land. I think about how You keep us warm in the winter, cool in the summer, and comfortable in the spring and early fall. Father, You always think of us. I thank You and praise Your name. You always know what we need 24/7. Creation responds to our needs through trees, leaves, grass, sun, moon, celestial stars, the air we breathe, and even the water we drink, which are all provided for us. The medicines that we take, the rest that we receive, the blessings upon blessings that You pour on us are too numerous to count. It never rains too much, the sun never shines too hot, the storms are never too hard, the valleys are never too deep, and the mountains are never too steep. You always bring us through. You always know what's best for us. Thank You, God, for 101° today. Thank You, God, for another hot day.

In Jesus' name. Amen.

A CLOUDY DAY

But as they sailed He fell asleep. And a windstorm came down on the lake, and they were filling with water, and were in jeopardy.
~ Luke 8:23 (NKJV)

Lord, thank You for this beautiful cloudy day. One that You sent for us to slow down, unwind, and know that You give us each day, with its problems and solutions. We know the sun is shining above the clouds. You are God when it is cloudy, and You are still God when it is raining. You are God when it is night and the same God when it is day. You are God when everything is excellent and the same God when it seems that everything is bad. You are an everyday, all-the-time God who never leaves us alone. We can count on You, our Father, Savior, Friend, and constant Companion. Every day with You is a wonderful day, cloudy or bright. We are never alone.

In Jesus' name. Amen.

A GIFT OF VEGETABLES

Therefore I remind you to stir up the gift of God which is in you through the laying on of my hands. ~ 2 Tim. 1:6 (NKJV)

Father God, thank You for a great surprise today. Rosie, a wonderful young lady who is a friend of my son, Curtis, came by today and surprised us with lots of green vegetables. They were so beautiful, and they looked so delicious. I was very appreciative that she thought of us. God bless young women like Rosie who think of their elders and gift them with vegetables or other necessary items. She called and she said, "Are you at home?" and I responded, "Yes." She said, "Well, come to the door." I went to the door, and she was standing there with the vegetables. Thank You, Father.

Rosie has been in the family for a long time. She's like a daughter, not by blood. She is a daughter by the blood of Jesus and the love of Jesus. Thank You, Father, for putting Rosie in my life. I know I can depend on her. I can call her, and she will come. Father, my heart is overjoyed when I think of young women like Rosie. Young women who have gone through the struggle. Young women who have learned to trust in You and know that You are the God of their salvation and have assurance that they can depend on You. I know there is no other but You who brought them through. I thank You for their learning, for their struggles, and their faith in a God Who always rescues and delivers. In Jesus' name, I ask You, Lord, to continue Your blessings on young women who are struggling but learning how to depend on You more.

In Jesus' name, I pray. Amen.

A PRAYER FOR OUR NATION

He will fulfill the desire of those who fear Him; He also will hear their cry and save them. ~ Ps. 145:19 (NKJV)

Father God, I thank You for the United States of America. I thank You for President Biden. God, though he is the head of the nation, You oversee the United States and the world.

Lord, we need Your help. The enemy has raised his head and has called for an insurrection in our nation. People have come across the United States to storm the capital. They are bearing arms and running over people, pushing the guards around, and threatening the lives of all whom they encounter. Lord, such ungodly behavior has never been experienced in my lifetime.

Father, we have always exercised some semblance of moral authority and a deep respect for the country. The United States of America has experienced significant turmoil: war after war between nations, families, civilians, and political parties; it's just too much going on. There is too much inequality in these states that are supposedly united. Too much attention is paid to the disparity in power between the two political parties. There are too many millionaires in this country who do not consider people who have basic needs, such as shelter, food, medicine, clothing, and care from others.

The enemy is loose, Father, and he's attacking Your people. I plead the blood of Jesus over the enemy and over all in this world. I truly believe, God, that You are in control and You hear the cries of Your people. I believe that justice and equality will reign in my lifetime. Let it be so, God, if it's Your *will*; let it be so.

In the name of Jesus. Amen.

A WEDNESDAY OF THANKSGIVING

Oh, give thanks to the Lord, for He is good! For His mercy endures forever. ~ Ps. 107:1 (NKJV)

Good morning, Almighty Father of *heaven* and *earth*! Thank You for this beautiful day of Thanksgiving. Thank You for the trees, naked and dressed. Thank You for the greening of the grass. We praise You for all the creatures scampering on the lawn and those flying in the air. Thank You for all the life surrounding me this morning. Thank You for this day and all that it brings to me. I am not in any way concerned or perplexed. You are with me all the time.

In the name of Jesus, thank You. Amen.

AMAZING GOD

And the Word became flesh and dwelt among us, and we beheld His glory, the glory as of the only begotten of the Father, full of grace and truth. ~ John 1:14 (NKJV)

On July 10th at approximately 7:45 PM in the year 2024, I saw Your glory shining all around my house and the sky. The glow was unbelievable. I called my husband, and we stood in awe as we looked at the colors. I walked outside and saw the trees; above the trees and all around, as far as the eye could see, was a beautiful glow. It was more gorgeous than I had ever seen before. I don't know if I will ever see it again, but I saw it today, God. I stood in awe, how amazing You are.

As I stood in my solarium and looked at the sky, it was glowing an amber color, one that I had seen before, but not in creation, not the glow that I had seen yesterday. I know there's some astrological explanation, perhaps that men can make. You, God, oversee the firmament and all of creation. Possibly my attempt to explain it is inadequate, but I saw You, in Your glory, surrounding me. The peace that followed was unbelievable. I love You, God. I know you, Father. You are just amazing.

In the name of Jesus. Amen.

EVENING SHADOWS FALLING ACROSS THE SKY

This was the Lord's doing; It is marvelous in our eyes.
~ Ps. 118:23 (NKJV)

Thank You, Father, for a beautiful day. The evening shadows are falling across the sky, and I see the beauty all around me. What a lovely scene! The tall trees, short trees, bushes, and the undergrowth are growing together, lifting their limbs toward the heavens, as if to say thank You, God, for one more day.

The blades of grass stand tall as if ready to receive some bounty that You are about to drop just for them. As I looked, Lord, I saw the squirrels and the rabbits, Your little creatures, scampering around looking for their evening meal. Some are just playing, enjoying where they are—enjoying Your provisions for each one of them.

I, too, join creation, thanking You, not only for the day, but for the evening shadows that are falling across the sky. It appears that the world is at peace; no disharmony, no trouble anywhere in the universe.

Where I am right now, God, I thank You for the serenity, for the peace, for the joy that passes all understanding. I'm here with You, a part of Your creation, and loving every bit of it.

In Jesus' name. Amen.

FAITHFUL FATHER

But you have an anointing from the Holy One, and you know all things. ~ 1 John 2:20 (NKJV)

God of our fathers, Your mighty hand holds us, guides, shields, comforts, lifts, and moves us. Father, You always forgive us, love us, and empower us. You encourage us, heal our wounds, dry our tears, wipe our eyes, carry our burdens, speak to us, speak through us, and assure us. God, You are so faithful. You walk with us, provide escape routes for us, console us, and even provide food when we are hungry. There is none like You, Father. You provide shelter during the storm, strength when we are weak, light in the darkest hour, and open doors for us. Father God, when we are lost and cannot find our way, You are right there. God, You are so faithful. Thank You for being our God.

In Jesus' name. Amen

GOD, MY EVERYTHING

I will instruct you and teach you in the way you should go; I will guide you with My eye. ~ Ps. 32:8 (NKJV)

Thank You, God, for providing for me and my family, as well as all the people I know and those I do not know. Thank You for the food on my table, the clothes on my back, the breath in my body, my vision (despite Macular Degeneration), my youngest daughter's new home, my oldest son's new contracts for his business, my youngest son's new apartment, my middle daughter's new car, my niece's new home, my oldest niece mortgage-free home, and for my nephew's new home. For all the provisions You make for my entire family.

I thank You for Macular Degeneration. I stand in awe of You! If I had a thousand tongues, I could not thank You enough for all that You do for us.

In Jesus' name. Amen.

GOOD MORNING, FATHER

This is the day the Lord has made; We will rejoice and be glad in it.
~ Ps. 118:24 (NKJV)

Thank You, God, for this beautiful, dreary, quiet Monday morning. Thank You for my husband, family, and friends. You woke us this morning with our right minds and the ability to call Your name. Thank You for being such a good God, keeping us all night and giving us peace in our spirit and a sense of happiness in our souls, with glee in our eyes. God, I praise You.

This is another day that You have given us to work in the commercialized fields of our choice. You have given us today to represent You wherever we go, whatever we do and say, even what we think, and how we feel, as well as how we love. We represent You in this dark world. Thank You for using us, Father. May there always be a smile on our faces, love in our hearts, softness in our approach to others, gentleness in our speech, understanding, grace, and compassion in what we do for, as well as to, those around us. Thank You, Father, for another day, unlike any other.

In Jesus' name, I pray. Amen.

GRATEFUL HEART

Moreover He said to me: "Son of man, receive into your heart all My words that I speak to you, and hear with your ears. ~ Ezek. 3:10 (NKJV)

Creative God of the seasons of life, weather, conditions, and traditions; God of all peoples of the universe, we come before You with grateful hearts. We lift our hearts in praise for the worship experience this morning. Thank You for Your strong *word* delivered to us by Your servant, Brother James Beal.

Thank You for giving us a new heart. Thank You for cleansing us and making us ready for Your service. Thank You for giving us Your Spirit to dwell within us. Your indwelling Spirit makes us aware of Your desire for us to do good, to love mercy, and to walk humbly with our God.

We hear Your *word* for us today, Lord. We realize that in times like these, we need to lean on You, trust You, and know that, though times may be difficult, You are doing a new thing in us and for us. It is the same as in Ezekiel's time; people are engaging in unethical, immoral, and unjust actions. They are not listening for or to Your *word*. Thank You, Father, for forgiving us; we honestly do not know what we do. Thank You for Your strength.

In Jesus' name, I pray. Amen.

IN THE MID-NIGHT HOUR

But at midnight Paul and Silas were praying and singing hymns to God, and the prisoners were listening to them. ~ Acts 16:25 (NKJV)

In the midnight hour when I am all alone, I begin to think about the goodness of the Lord. All day, You have been by our side. Through moments of doubt, fear, indecision, hurt, and pain, You have been right beside each one of us.

Lord, I am so thankful for Your provisions, love, protection, grace, and mercy. In the midnight hour, I feel Your comfort and I know that You are with me. Thank You, Lord, for the midnight hour.

In the name of Jesus. Amen.

INSTRUCTING GOD OF NATURE

Lord, who may abide in Your tabernacle? Who may dwell in Your holy hill? ~ Ps. 15:1 (NKJV)

Father God, of Helen, Lorenza, C.O., Guy, Leroy, and millions of folks around the globe who died, and those who live, and are still learning and leaning on the *word* of life, we offer You praise. We thank You for always instructing us in Your *word* of life. Your *word* guides us to the truth spoken to power. Your Book of Life teaches us how to live in this jungle. We observe the trees, bushes, birds, and animals scampering on the ground, as well as bumblebees and yellow jackets competing for habitation. Nature in all its splendor is learning how to give and take, how to recognize differences, and yet use the space that God has given them to grow together in harmony, respect, and love. God, You are always instructing us to live a life that is pleasing to You and prosperous to us. My heart is filled with gratitude. You are always instructing us on how to live a life worthy of Christ, our Savior.

In the name of Jesus. Amen.

JESUS, THE PROPITIATOR

In this is love, not that we loved God, but that He loved us and sent His Son to be the propitiation for our sins. ~ 1 John 4:10 (NKJV)

Father, I come this morning with a heart filled with thanksgiving and a mouth overflowing with praise. Every organ, sinew, muscle, vein, artery, tissue, blood, body fluids, cells, molecules, and any other parts that I know not are functioning according to Your divine purpose.

Thank You, Father, for this day. A day that is filled with joys and celebrations. I celebrate You, Father. I am so thankful to know You for myself. My joy is knowing that I have a Father who oversees all that I do. The One who hears, listens, understands, forgives, and still loves me. Lord, I am so thankful.

In Jesus' name. Amen.

MAGNIFY THE LORD

Let all those who seek You rejoice and be glad in You; Let such as love Your salvation say continually, "The Lord be magnified!"
~ Ps. 40:16 (NKJV)

I magnify You, Lord, for You are worthy to be praised. I praise You for the beautiful cloudless day. I praise You for the warmth that surrounds me. I praise You for the gift of sight. Praise You for the ability to move about and be active in this magnificent world of Yours.

I praise You for the rising of the sun and the going down of the moon. I praise You for the rotation, the spinning, the turning of the earth and the planets, yet never colliding. I praise You for creation.

I magnify You for all You do in Your world with Your people. I lift You, God, as I see You working in the lives of people around the globe: the haves and the have-nots, the rich and the poor. I magnify You for the world we live in, and I magnify You for this wilderness that we navigate through for better or worse. You, O God, are worthy to be praised. I rejoice because I am Yours; I belong to You.

In Jesus' name, I pray. Amen.

OVERSEEING GOD

Brethren, if a man is overtaken in any trespass, you who are spiritual restore such a one in a spirit of gentleness, considering yourself lest you also be tempted. ~ Gal. 6:1 (NKJV)

God of the universe, God of creation, God of all there was, all there is, and all there will be, I greet You this morning as humbly as I know how. My soul is at peace, and my body feels well. My organs are working according to Your purpose; my mind is sound, and my heart is staying on You.

We are in the middle of a tornado. The wind is blowing, the rain is falling torrentially, and the tree limbs and leaves appear to be dancing with glee. My husband and I, along with our family, are inside, sheltered from the weather because of Your love and care for us. Thank You, Father, I know that You care for all in the universe, regardless of the situation. As I trust You when all is well, when the sun is shining, and it's a beautiful, warm, pleasant, or balmy day, I trust You in the middle of a tornado. You know far better than we do what we need to let go of and what we need to pick up. Thank You for it all, God.

In the name of Jesus. Amen.

PERFECT PEACE

Let him turn away from evil and do good; Let him seek peace and pursue it. ~ 1 Pet. 3:11 (NKJV)

God of this beautiful, bountiful universe, Creator of all there is or ever will be, with a grateful heart I come before You this morning. Praise is on my lips and in my heart and head. I am at peace in my body and my soul. Calmness seems to envelop my space, and my spirit is so light. Silence surrounds my home. I have no concerns because You are here. I feel Your presence. Thank You for taking up residence in this space.

Thank You for protecting my husband, children, grandchildren, great-grandchildren, nieces, nephews, aunts, uncles, grandparents, and relatives around the globe. We are all cousins. You began with two, and now we are too many to count. How great You are, Father. Thank You for perfect peace.

In Jesus' name. Amen.

PLEASING GOD

that you may walk worthy of the Lord, fully pleasing Him, being fruitful in every good work and increasing in the knowledge of God;
~ Col. 1:10 (NKJV)

Lord of all, to You I lift my voice in praise on this beautiful day of thanksgiving. My earnest desire is to please You today in every way. I want to please You in every move that I make and in every breath that I take. I want to represent You in loving my sisters and brothers, in my greetings, speaking, encouraging, and my prayers. I aim to be a blessing in my relationships by offering defense, patience, help, support, provision, and service. Thank You, God, for supporting me in my sitting down, getting up, departing, arriving, smiles, glances, and even the nodding of my head. Lord, let me please You. I want to walk in a manner worthy of my calling.

Lord, please strengthen me in doing what You would have me do. According to Your *word*, I will be fruitful in good works, and by doing so, I will grow in the knowledge of You, my God. Let me grow, please let me grow.

In Jesus' name. Amen.

POWER THROUGH PRAYER

But you shall receive power when the Holy Spirit has come upon you;
and you shall be witnesses to Me in Jerusalem, and in all Judea
and Samaria, and to the end of the earth." ~ Acts 1:8 (NKJV)

Gracious God Jehovah, thank You for the opportunity to come into Your presence with praise and thanksgiving. I thank You for giving me the chance to have conversations with You every day. Thank You, God, for empowering me with Your strength and power to speak the truth to power. Thank You for all that You have done.

It is in Your power that I move and have my being. It is in Your power that I'm able to reach out and help somebody. It is in Your power that I can cleave my tongue to the roof of my mouth when something is said that is unkind. Thank You, God, for Your power, strength, and rule in my life. It is through Your ruling me that I have the power through prayer to speak the truth in love.

In Jesus' name, I pray. Amen.

PRAISE THE LORD!

Let everything that has breath praise the Lord. Praise the Lord!
~ Ps. 150:6 (NKJV)

Thank You for making a way out of no way today. I ask You, Father, for the grass cutter to come before Mother's Day. I had misplaced the number, Father. You heard my prayer. The grass cutter arrived, and the lawn was manicured. Thank You, Father.

I was told from a young age to seek You on all matters. Father, I remember. Thank You for the teachings I received from the elders of the community. You, alone, are worthy to be praised. We pray, You hear, You answer, we believe, You resolve. Thank You, Father.

In the name of Jesus. Amen.

PRAY BELIEVING

Which is easier, to say, 'Your sins are forgiven you,' or to say, 'Rise up and walk'? [24] *But that you may know that the Son of Man has power on earth to forgive sins"—He said to the man who was paralyzed, "I say to you, arise, take up your bed, and go to your house."*
~ Luke 5:23-24 (NKJV)

We believe in You, Father; we believe in the Holy Trinity. We believe that Jesus died on the Cross for our sins, once and for all. We believe that He died for everybody. We believe that You love everybody. We believe that the Holy Spirit, the Comforter, is with us. We believe that You will never leave us. We believe that You always answer prayers. We believe that the blood of Jesus covers us. We believe that You lead us every day, every moment, and that You have all power. We believe that You desire a pure and contrite heart and want the best for each one of Your children.

We believe that there is a bright side somewhere. We believe that one day we will be in the place where the wicked will cease from troubling, and the weary will be at rest. We believe that one day all Your children will sit around the throne and be blessed.

Creation and all of life could not exist without You, Lord. Thank You, Lord, for hearing our prayers, unuttered or expressed.

In Jesus' name, I pray. Amen.

TALKING TO JESUS

By this we know that we abide in Him, and He in us, because He has given us of His Spirit. ~ 1 John 4:13 (NKJV)

When your burdens seem too heavy to bear, talk to Jesus. When you cannot find a hiding place, when your spouse is not being kind, when you are lost, when you cannot get a breakthrough, when it seems like the world is tossing you, when the debts are piling up, when your finances are not enough for the family, when the rent is due, when the medical opinions are grave, when you cannot see the light at the end of the tunnel; I tell you, it is time to have a little talk with Jesus and tell Him all about your problems.

The saints told me, "He will hear your faintest cry, and He will answer." I tell you, you will feel Him in your heart, and you will know that He hears and talks to you. Talking with Jesus makes everything alright.

In Jesus' name. Amen.

TELL ME AGAIN, FATHER

Most assuredly, I say to you, We speak what We know and testify
what We have seen, and you do not receive Our witness.
~ John 3:11 (NKJV)

Father, strengthen me to be bold and speak truth to power in the name of Jesus and to tell of Your glory and power and to tell of Your goodness and what You have done for me in the last few days.

My left arm was numb for two and a half days before I went to the Emergency Department at Johns Hopkins Hospital. The EKGs, Echo Cardiograms, MRIs, EEG, and CATH scans were taken of my heart, brain, and cervical spine to rule out heart attack or strokes and pinched nerves. The results were negative.

Thank You, Father, for the healing before I arrived at the hospital. The physicians determined that, due to the narrowing of the space between the vertebrae, physical therapy would be necessary. You answered my prayers for wholeness. Let me speak to what I know, and testify to what I have seen, that others may believe my witness.

In the name of Jesus. Amen.

THANK YOU FOR BEING MY GOD

And my spirit has rejoiced in God my Savior. ~ Luke 1:47 (NKJV)

Father God, Healer and Deliver, Savior of all humankind, my joy and my peace; that's who You are to me. Thank You, God, for being my God. You are so wonderful, kind, and loving. You care for me when I often forget about myself or my health. You cause all my organs to obey You and work according to Your purpose. You keep my flesh sensitive to the outside environment. You restore my soul. God, You lead me through dark passages. When I often find myself afraid, I remember that You are with me. When I find myself perplexed over issues of life, the evil that men place upon men causes tears to fall, my heart begins to yearn, and then I remember, this is my Father's world. When I feel as if I can't go on, I remember what Jesus did on Calvary, and I draw strength from the power You send to me to go further. The breath that I breathe, the ability to see beyond myself, the food that I am allowed to eat, the movement that I make, everything about me depends on You, Father. Thank You, God, for being my God, my Father, my beginning, and my end. You, God, are my power. I love You. I magnify Your name.

In the name of Jesus, my Lord and my Savior. I thank You, God, for being my God. Amen.

THANK YOU, GOD, FOR ONE MORE DAY.

Therefore do not worry about tomorrow, for tomorrow will worry about its own things. Sufficient for the day is its own trouble.
~ Matt. 6:34 (NKJV)

My life is so good, Father. As I think about the goodness of the Lord and what You have done for me and my family, my heart rejoices, and my soul is lifted. I praise You for this beautiful day. The bright sunshine warming up creation, the breeze in the air letting us know that You hold everything in Your hand, controls the air that we breathe, the light that surrounds us, and the darkness that often enfold us.

I thank You, Father, for this day and for all that has occurred: the walk in the park for the exercise of my body, the pedicure, and the manicure that I was able to receive with quietness and serenity. For the ability to assist someone who has found herself without a home. Thank You, Father, for blessing me so abundantly that I'm able to help another one of our sisters along the way. You are so good and kind, and my heart overflows when I think about Your goodness. Thank You, God, for one more day and one more opportunity to do Your *will*.

In Jesus' name, we pray. Amen.

THE ACTIVITY OF OUR BRAIN

And do not be conformed to this world, but be transformed by the renewing of your mind, that you may prove what is that good and acceptable and perfect will of God. ~ Rom. 12:2 (NKJV)

Thank You, God, for the beauty of this day. You blessed us with the activity of our brain and the movement of our limbs. Thank You that our organs are performing as You designed them. You, Father, allow us to walk and work in Your service today. You blessed us to be able to speak to others about Your goodness and tender mercies toward us.

Thank You, God, for another opportunity, for Your blessing of strength to try to obey Your *will*.

In the name of Jesus, I pray. Amen.

THE GOODNESS OF GOD

Oh, how great is Your goodness, Which You have laid up for those who fear You, Which You have prepared for those who trust in You In the presence of the sons of men! ~ Ps. 31:19 (NKJV)

Good morning, Divine Redeemer. Thank You for a beautiful day. Thank You for the bright sunshine and the chill that is in the air. Your goodness is too much for me to comprehend. You are so good and kind. You lead us through the valleys day by day. You guide us through conversations, both in our work and in our play. You have held and led me all my life. Thank You, this morning. Your goodness is so vast and so wonderful. I give You praise, God, for Your goodness unto me.

In the name of Jesus. Amen.

THE NIGHTTIME IS THE RIGHT TIME

For this cause everyone who is godly shall pray to You In a time when You may be found; Surely in a flood of great waters They shall not come near him. ~ Ps. 32:6 (NKJV)

Father God, thank You. Nighttime is the right time to talk with Jesus and share my concerns. Thank You for the opportunity, dear God. The sun is setting, and I'm exhausted, but I'm also thankful to get into my warm bed shortly. Father God, I love and appreciate You, and I thank You for being with me throughout the day.

Thank You for keeping me safe from hurt, harm, and danger. I praise You for healing my knee, dear God. I did not have to take any narcotics. I love You, Lord, and I just thank You because You've been so good and kind. You've been with me, and not just with me, but with all the people of the universe. I'm thankful for what You've done for me and my family today.

Thank You for my grandson, who is not having any difficulty in his job and who seems to be conforming and doing what is expected of him. Thank You, God, for my great-grandson, who is just learning to navigate the waters of his school and has discovered friends with whom he can play. Thank You, God, he wants to bring his friends home with him. What a fantastic idea. He's thinking of his friends and how he loves them, and wants to continue being with them. He likes the fellowship, thank You, God.

We love You, Lord. You're doing a great thing. I know that nighttime is the right time for me to come and bare my soul to You, and You understand. Thank You, Father, for Your understanding, powerful love, devotion, protection, and support in this wilderness.

In Jesus' name, I pray. Amen.

THE POWER OF CHRIST

And He said to me, "My grace is sufficient for you, for My strength is made perfect in weakness." Therefore most gladly I will rather boast in my infirmities, that the power of Christ may rest upon me.
~ 2 Cor. 12:9 (NKJV)

Father, I thank You for allowing my husband, who is 90 years old, to cut the front lawn today. You gave him energy, strength, vision, coordination of his limbs, and a mind filled with amazement at the wonder of creation. I praise You for the 3 acres of beautiful grass. God, You are so powerful. You always know what is best for us. You made it possible for him to be gifted, by our children, with an electric lawn mower. He loves the silence as he mows the lawn. It is a time when he can have a little talk with You. You made it possible for him to get his exercise without driving 30 miles to the Columbia Mall for his walk. You always ensure that your children receive the best benefits. Lord, I just thank You.

In the name of Jesus. Amen.

WORKING TOGETHER

We know that all things work together for good[a] for those who love God, who are called according to his purpose. ~ Rom. 8:28 (NRSVA)

Good morning, Father. Thank You for this beautiful day in which You have given me to rejoice, to make a difference, and to be glad. Thank You for every organ in my body working together according to Your purpose. This frame, in which I travel, feels good today. I honor You; Thank You for blessing and covering me with Your love.

God, I feel good knowing that You are with me. You guide me, and You keep me in perfect peace. May all that I do today honor You and please You. You get all the glory and honor, for I am Yours.

In the name of Jesus. Amen.

YOU, LORD, GAVE US POWER

Then Jesus summoned his twelve disciples and gave them authority over unclean spirits, to cast them out, and to cure every disease and every sickness. ~ Matt. 10:1 (NRSVA)

O blessed Father of the universe, I come to You with a grateful heart for today's blessings. I read, understand, and believe Your *word*, which is nourishment for my soul. Just like You gave the disciples power, I believe that Your Spirit, working through me, can cast out unclean spirits. Because I believe, I claim You and Your power to work through me to help my sister regain strength in her upper body. I declare and decree that the demonic spirit that holds her has no control. Whatever she had is over! I plead the blood over her and her whole body, right now! I plead it in the name of God and her Brother, Savior, and Deliverer, Jesus the Christ.

All glory be Yours, Father, now and forever. Amen.

5

THE POWER OF GOD

A GLIMPSE OF HEAVEN

And immediately, coming up [a]from the water, He saw the heavens [b]parting and the Spirit descending upon Him like a dove.
~ Mark 1:10 (NKJV)

My Lord, what a beautiful day You gave us. Your sun is shining brightly, the warm rays filling the atmosphere and making everyone want to get outside and experience life. Children are running and playing. Adults are walking, greeting one another with nods of the head, warm smiles, and communicating with each other. You blessed us with a glimpse of heaven today, Father. Peace, joy, happiness, contentment, understanding, and people helping each other carry groceries, crossing the street, and giving a helping hand. I exclaimed, "Look at God," working in us today. Only You, Lord, can control Your world, only You.

In the name of Jesus. Amen.

ALL THINGS WORK TOGETHER

And we know that all things work together for good to those who love God, to those who are the called according to His purpose.
~ Rom. 8:28 (NKJV)

Father, my nephew is a good man. He is faithful and true to You. He has raised his daughter in the church. She, too, has strong faith. The financial burden of the surgery for her kidney transplant was too much for him to bear. Amid financial difficulties, the enemy attacked him. My nephew grew weak; his faith was shaken; he yielded to the enemy.

The enemy is a liar. My nephew belongs to the great God, Jehovah. God is his *sustainer, deliverer, healer*, and *provider*. God can and will bring my nephew and his daughter through this storm of life. I believe Father, that all things do work together for good to those who love You, to those who are called according to Your purpose. I know You will work it out, Father.

In the name of Jesus. Amen.

CLEANSE THE HEART OF JEALOUSY

Then I will give them one heart, and I will put a new spirit within [a] them, and take the stony heart out of their flesh, and give them a heart of flesh, that they may walk in My statutes and keep My judgments and do them; and they shall be My people, and I will be their God.
~ *Ezek. 11:19-20 (NKJV)*

Thank You, God, for family. Thank You for the love, togetherness, and the feeling of being connected to those who love You. Thank You for family, from generations past to the present moment. You always provide what we need and our desires have been filled with Your love, care, and Your presence. Father, You have richly given to us abundant food, clothing, a wonderful home, friends, education, and celebrations.

We have had family gatherings and great Christmases, sharing gifts in remembrance of the greatest gift that has ever been given. The family celebrates every birthday and achievements of each child. You have provided us with opportunities to demonstrate by reaching out and sharing with others who have been less fortunate. Yet, jealousy seems to take over one of our children.

Father, I pray in the name of Jesus for that ungodly spirit to be removed from my child. It serves no purpose but to destroy the person and the family by breaking down relationships and causing separation. I love them all and I pray for deliverance. Only You can remove the spirit of jealousy. Only You, Lord, can cleanse the heart of this evil spirit: only You, Lord, only You.

In the name of Jesus. Amen.

FATHER ALONE

Come to Me, all you who labor and are heavy laden, and I will give you rest. ~ Matt. 11:28 (NKJV)

Good evening, Father. I thank You for this day of joy, peace, and love. Thank You for the mercy You have shown to all. This day has been filled with news of the illnesses of Diane, Sammy, James, and Gloria. Father, You alone know the depths of their condition. You alone are the *healer*. You alone love each of us too deeply to lose any one of us. I call on the only One that I know that can calm the sea, move a mountain, and open doors that no man can open. I call on the only One who can take care of this world and all its inhabitants. It is You, Father. It is always You.

In the name of Jesus. Amen.

GOD, MY HEALER

Who forgives all your iniquities, Who heals all your diseases, ~ Ps. 103:3 (NKJV)

Father God, I know You are the *healer*. I have history with You. I know You for myself. You healed my mother, Helen; Aunt Lorenza; grandmother, Daisy; grandfather, Jack; and grandfather, Gus. You told each one of them to go on just a little longer. I thank You, Father, because You do it repeatedly. I thank You, Father, for my cousin Frances's improved health and my daughter's successful surgery. Nine hours, You worked through the surgeons for her wholeness. Thank You, Father, for healing my cousin, Jackie, from cancer and her husband, Robert, from permanent spinal damage, and Greta from a heart attack.

"Thank You, Almighty God, for all that You have done and are doing for my family right now.

In the name of Jesus. Amen.

GOD, MY SUPPLIER

And my God shall supply all your need according to His riches in glory by Christ Jesus. ~ Phil. 4:19 (NKJV)

My gracious and masterful Father, my heart is filled with joy this morning as I look up into the sky and imagine what my mother and father, stepfather, grandparents, aunts, uncles, and others who have gone are doing in heaven today. I know that they are happy and are cheering us on.

They are with *"the supplier"* of all our needs: the *one* who keeps us from falling; walks in front of us; always takes care of us; *who* guides our feet while we wander through the wilderness; knows each one of us by name; and the *one who* is always aware of our needs. Father, I recognize and I am so thankful for all You do for me and my family.

In Jesus' name. Amen.

GOD OF ABUNDANCE
Part 1

And God is able to make all grace abound toward you, that you, always having all sufficiency in all things, may have an abundance for every good work. ~ 2 Cor. 9:8 (NKJV)

Creative, *holy*, *righteous*, and *good* God, You are the giver of every good and perfect gift to me. I thank You for Your goodness and all the blessings that You pour out on me repeatedly. Father, You bless every one of Your children. The vastness of Your blessings, love, grace, and mercy is too immense for us to comprehend. You provide us with food on the table, water to drink, shelter, and You've furnished that shelter so that we have enough space for ourselves, families, and friends. Father, You provide everything that we could need. You're such a wonderful Father. Thank You for Your provisions, love, and care toward us.

In Jesus' name, I pray. Amen.

GOD OF ABUNDANCE
Part 2

And God is able to make all grace abound toward you, that you, always having all sufficiency in all things, may have an abundance for every good work. ~ 2 Cor. 9:8 (NKJV)

This morning, Holy God of creation, I have a grateful heart and a mouth filled with praise. A retirement celebration was held for me on Saturday, June 29, 2024, by the Staff Pastor Parish Relations Ministry of West Liberty United Methodist Church in Marriottsville, Maryland. God, I am so grateful for the work that was done to celebrate my ministry with this church. Clergy and laity working together for God has always been and will always be my theme. Father, You received much praise, for all belongs to You. You work through me for the good of Your people. I am one of Your children, and when You speak through me, You are also talking to me. I thank You, God, for this pastorate of 15 years. It's been an incredible journey. I have seen a transformation in the people who worship there. I have seen people who were too intimidated to pray become willing to pray. I have seen people who initially thought they should not read the scripture in the service become willing to read and participate in the worship experience. They are now quoting and interpreting scriptures, and trying to live by Your *word*.

I thank You, God, my heart is filled with an abundance of grace, praise, mercy, and faithfulness to You. Almighty God, You show me a glimpse of heaven now and then. Thank You, God, for the experience that brings so much joy.

In Jesus' name. Amen.

GOD OF ABUNDANCE
Part 3

And God is able to make all grace abound toward you, that you, always having all sufficiency in all things, may have an abundance for every good work. ~ 2 Cor. 9:8 (NKJV)

Thank You, Father, for a wonderful worship experience on Sunday, June 30, 2024. The praise team was terrific. The Spirit was high, and we felt the presence of the Lord. The testimonies were filled with joy as people shared how God had intervened in their lives, addressing their problems just a few weeks prior. The testimonies were filled with grace and mercy, and as one person spoke, others were encouraged to share their stories, one after the other. You were there, God.

The message, entitled "You Know What to Do, Just Do Right!," was filled with words encouraging us to move forward and leave the past behind. Not to let the past take the joy of the presence away, not to let the past steal the freedom that we have received through the forgiving grace of God. It was my last service at West Liberty Church. Everything and everyone was filled with the Holy Spirit. The songs were sufficient and appropriate. One of the songs was by Jessie Dixon, "I Got Leaving on My Mind," which flooded my soul with tears.

I exited the church on the Postlude "The Goodness of God," by C. C. Wyman, with head bowed, body bent, and tears flowing. It was my last time serving as Senior Pastor in the Baltimore-Washington Conference of the UMC. Thank You, God, for the experience.

In Jesus' name, I pray. Amen.

GOD OF THE DAWNING

"Immediately after the tribulation of those days the sun will be darkened, and the moon will not give its light; the stars will fall from heaven, and the powers of the heavens will be shaken. ~ Matt. 24:29 (NKJV)

God of life, liberty, justice, peace, honor, glory, and dominion over the universe, here I am again. This morning marks the dawning of a new day, a new time in the lives of the Sands family. There is a lump in my chest, a heaviness in my walk, sadness in my voice, and a downness in my spirit. It is a time of heaviness in my soul. Lord, I know You to be a bridge over troubled waters, an anchor in the middle of the ocean, a shelter in the times of a storm, and a *way maker* when there is no way. All my faith is in You. You, *who* make no mistake. You, *who* know us better than we know ourselves. You, *who* have been with us for years. You know what we need.

Lord, we need another blessing from You. A healing for Robin Yvonne Robinson Sands: from fingertip to fingertip, from the top of her head to the soles of her feet. Please, Father, let Robin see the dawning of a new day, if it is in Your *will*, then let it be so.

In Jesus' name. Amen.

GOD OF THE DAY

This is the day the Lord has made; We will rejoice and be glad in it.
~ Ps.118:24 (NKJV)

Friend of the friendless, God, of our weary years, You have brought us to this day. Father, with grateful hearts, we come to You today. It is a rainy, cloudy day, a day filled with swift transitions, a day that some would call dreary. I called it another day that You have made for us to rejoice and to be glad.

God, You are our *helper* and *deliverer*, regardless of the weather. You are the God of the wind, rain, storms, and snow, cloudy, and cloudless days. You are the God of all forever, whatever the day might bring.

I'm so thankful to know that I have You as a friend who sticks closer than any brother, a Father who is always with me. I thank You, God, for each day that You allow me to be on this side of Jordan.

Thank You, Father, in Jesus' name. Amen.

GOD OF VIRGINS

And behold, you will conceive in your womb and bring forth a Son, and shall call His name Jesus. ~ Luke 1:31 (NKJV)

Holy God of all people, You are so great and powerful. Only You could decide to have the Holy Spirit impregnate a virgin, have her conceive, and bring forth the Savior of the world. An unknown girl from a small, poor country, whose mother, a spiritual woman, raised her daughter in the faith. How great You are, Father. You gave her an experience of a lifetime. An angel spoke and informed her of all that would happen. Her response was, "I am a maidservant of the Lord. Let it be to me according to Your *word*."

God of virgins, thank You for Jesus. Amen.

GOD, OUR DELIVERER

O wretched man that I am! Who will deliver me from this body of death? ~ Rom. 7:24 (NKJV)

Good morning, Creator of the universe. Thank You for waking me this morning to a day that looks like it may storm. I need You, Father. I am so full of sorrow for my son, Curtis. It seems like he does not want to get rid of the dependency on illegal drugs. Father, I have cried and prayed; prayed and cried. I know You are the Deliverer; I know You are the only Savior that he has. I know You can if You want to. He once said to me, "Mom, I must want to get off drugs. I will when I am ready. It's just too hard right now." I know he is Your child, Lord. I know You will deliver him when You are ready. I trust You, Lord. Your *will*, Father, is what I seek.

In Jesus' name. Amen.

GOD, OUR MAKER

Truly, this only I have found: That God made man upright, But they have sought out many schemes." ~ Eccles.. 7:29 (NKJV)

Father, this wilderness is filled with so many transitions. I pray for the world to remember who You are. Life seems to have no value, no importance, and no meaning to many people who are determined to harm others in any way possible. I am looking at the news, and the world has been notified that there has been another mass shooting. Today, at the University of Nevada, six students were shot. Father God, please protect the students, calm their spirits, and soothe their bodies. Be with the parents, faculty, and all others who are worried right now. Strengthen us to be stronger witnesses of Your goodness, power, presence, and love.

In Jesus' name, I pray. Amen.

GOD, THE PROBLEM SOLVER

Be anxious for nothing, but in everything by prayer and supplication,
with thanksgiving, let your requests be made known to God;
~ Phil. 4:6 (NKJV)

God of today and every day of every life, I approach You this morning in awe of Your strength and power. I listen to the news and see trouble everywhere in the world.

Today, one of the former presidents is wreaking havoc around the world. Everybody is in an uproar. It seems that folk do not know what to do or where to turn. I know *who* has the answer and the solution to the problems. We must bring our problems to You. You, Father, handle world and personal problems. God, You are the great problem solver. The songwriter states, "Take your burdens to the Lord and leave them there." We cannot solve anything like You can.

God, You are the answer and the solution. My trust is in You, and I believe in You. Thank You, God, for solving every one of my problems.

In Jesus' name. Amen.

GOD'S ARMS OF LOVE

bears all things, believes all things, hopes all things, endures all things.
~ 1 Cor. 13:7 (NKJV)

Father of all masses of land, wind, and fire, we acknowledge that all power and wisdom are from You. Thank You for all that this day brought before me. I thank You for the strength, guidance, comfort, security, and serenity that You give me. I felt Your presence all day, Father. I give You praise, Father. I trust and believe in You completely. You provide for all Your children. Thank You for surrounding us with Your arms of love.

In the name of Jesus. Amen.

HARM AND DANGER

And who is he who will harm you if you become followers of what is good? ~ 1 Pet. 3:13 (NKJV)

My Father and Guardian of life, this is Your child, B. J. Sands, again. I am so grateful for another day to try to do what You expect me to do. Father, life is so fragile, and the works of the ungodly spirits are ever before me, attempting to conquer my soul. I hear Your voice telling me to "hold on."

Thank You, Father, for keeping me out of the snares of evil, jealousy, greed, deceivers, and workers of iniquity. Thank You for Your constant presence. Thank You for keeping me on solid ground. Thank You for keeping my soul anchored in You. Thank You for the Holy Spirit surrounding and comforting me when the stressors of life seem to attack my body. Thank You for reminding me that I am a follower of all that is good. Your *word* tells me that "Tho they slay me, yet will I trust in You." You are all that is good. Everything good and perfect comes from You, Father. Thank You for accepting me as Yours and keeping me out of harm's way and danger.

In Jesus' name. Amen.

HELP IN TROUBLE

God is our refuge and strength, A very present help in trouble.
~ Ps. 46:1 (NKJV)

Father, I lift before You, my son, Curtis. He remains troubled after all these years. He knows You for himself. He trusts You. He knows Your strength, and yet, he has allowed Satan to have such a hold on him that he will not let go.

Lord, in the name of Jesus, I plead the blood of Jesus over my son and all his friends. I believe that God has all power. My God does not force anyone to come to Him, yet He waits for each one of us.

I pray for my son to hold on to his faith, and to hold on to that which he knows in his heart to be true, while holding God's unchanging hand. Father, You are the only *one* to release him from the bonds of Satan. I cast out all demons right now. Hold on. Help is on the way.

In the name of Jesus. Amen.

HIS PRESENCE IN THE ROOM

You will show me the path of life; In Your presence is fullness of joy; At Your right hand are pleasures forevermore. ~ Ps. 16:11 (NKJV)

Father God, thank You, I'm standing on Your promises. I believe in Your *word*, God. Thank You for strengthening me to walk all over my house today. The surgery on Friday the 13th was successful. God, as I prayed with the doctors and medical personnel assisting in my procedure, one could feel Your presence in the room. We felt Your blessings, and there was praise in the room.

I reflected on that as I was waiting for them to carry me back to the operating room, and I said, "This room of preparation has become a Chapel today." The name of the Lord was lifted. My heart was filled with joy and praise; my spirit was high, and my physical being felt well. I said to myself, "All is well with my soul. You're a great and wonderful God. I can count on You. I trust You, and I know You will bring me through this storm today."

In Jesus' name, I pray. Amen.

HOLD ON TO THE PROMISE

For all the promises of God in Him are Yes, and in Him Amen, to the glory of God through us. ~ 2 Cor. 1:20 (NKJV)

Father, You promised that You would be our God, *provider*, and *deliverer*. Holy Spirit, You promised to be our *guide*. Jesus, You promised that You would be our Savior and our *friend*. You also promised that You would stick closer than any brother.

Thank You, Triune God. In You, I have all that I will ever need. I am standing on Your promises. I cannot fail. I believe in Your *words*. I have faith in You. You will see me through the wilderness of life, every struggle, storm, situation, and every attack of the enemy will fail. I will hold on to the promises.

In the name of Jesus. Amen.

HOLY QUIETNESS

Whoever is wise will observe these things, And they will understand the lovingkindness of the Lord. ~ Ps. 107:43 (NKJV)

Lord of all, Creator of the universe, my heavenly Father, thank You for holy quietness. Last night, You spoke to us through the wind and the rain. We felt Your presence. You spoke from 9:13 AM to 8:30 PM yesterday. We saw the raindrops falling like a curtain. We could not see our neighbor's house. We witnessed Your glory as the wind blew and the leaves on the trees and the trees themselves all moved in awe of Your presence, and yet there was no fear, for You were showing Your power and letting the world know *who* is in charge of the universe.

You woke us this morning to a bright, sunny, cloudless day. We stand in awe of Your glory, Father. The wind is blowing very hard. You are drying the land that surrounds us, Father. Only You can bring peace and holy quietness in the middle and after a storm. Speak to us, Creator. We are listening.

In Jesus' name. Amen.

I SEE YOU IN THE WORLD

The Lord shall preserve your going out and your coming in From this time forth, and even forevermore ~ Ps. 121:8 (NKJV)

Wonderful God and Savior of the world, I see You in my mind's eye: a baby placed in a manger, in the cold of winter, kept warm by the breath of farm animals standing around in amazement. I see Your circumcision in the temple. I see You at the age of 12 talking to the elders and teaching them in the temple. Savior, I see You as You walked among the people, showing them the *way*. I see You healing the blind, the crippled, the deranged, the sinners, the backsliders. I see You helping all the people. I see You walking with the fishermen. I see You teaching and preaching to the disciples; I see You with all the world's people, trying to show us how to get it right.

Thank You, Savior, for never giving up. As You have been doing since You came into this world, You are still doing today.

In Jesus' name. Amen.

LAST NIGHT'S HEALING

If you abide in Me, and My words abide in you, you will ask what you desire, and it shall be done for you. ~ John 15:7 (NKJV)

Healing God, thank You for the healing You provided for those who needed it last night. God, my healing needed to take place in my large intestine. I ate chocolate-covered peanuts and drank a strawberry milkshake. I knew that it was the wrong thing to do, but I said my grace and ate what I knew I should not eat because I was hungry. Father, despite my waywardness, You healed me last night. When the pain was unbearable, I called on You, and You answered my prayers. Thank You, God.

Again, You allowed me to see with my spiritual eyes that all I had to do was be patient a little longer, and I would have the food necessary for the day. Forgive my disobedience, God. Forgive me for doing what I wanted to do rather than what I was supposed to do. You showed me an example in life: when we rely on our own understandings and actions, we suffer the consequences. Thank You for Your demonstration again, Father. Thank You for healing me. I trust and I love You, and I know You always know what's right for me. I pray with a humble heart and a contrite spirit.

In Jesus' name. Amen.

MEDICAL STAFF WHO ARE BELIEVERS

For with the heart one believes unto righteousness, and with the mouth confession is made unto salvation. For the Scripture says, "Whoever believes on Him will not be put to shame." ~ Rom. 10:10-11 (NKJV)

Lord, thank You for the good news. Today I went in for my annual cardiology visit. Lord, I asked You to please be with the doctor and give him the wisdom he needed to ensure everything was well with my heart.

Father, I was questioned by the nurse and the physician's assistant. I was so pleased with them as they asked how it is between You and me. Father, I told him how it was between me and You. I shared how I trust and love You, and how You've been working with me and through me. I shared with them how You delivered me just this week. My lungs are functioning well; I had no asthma or allergy attacks, and everything was fine. I give You praise for wellness. The physician's assistant said, "I can count on you telling me about God the Creator." I replied, "He's the only *one* I know. He's the *one* in charge. He's the *one* who keeps us, me and you, doing what we do in the name of Jesus.

Thank You, Father, for doctors, nurses, and physicians' assistants who are true believers in the *one living* God. I love You, Lord; all is well. My report regarding my heart was excellent. Thank You, Father.

In the name of Jesus. Amen.

ON-TIME GOD

For this cause everyone who is godly shall pray to You In a time when You may be found; Surely in a flood of great waters They shall not come near him. ~ Ps. 32:6 (NKJV)

Father, You are an On-Time God. Thank You for always making a way for us. Yesterday, July 10, my husband was locked out of the house. The code would not work, so he was unable to get into the house. Just this morning, the code was working briefly, but then we couldn't get in or out. But, God, You always make a way.

God, You did it again for us. I called A. J., the owner of a house repair business. I call every time there's a problem. Every time I call, he makes a way to get to me as soon as possible. This morning at 10:55, he called to see if there was anything I needed before he went on vacation. I informed him that the locks on the front and rear doors were not functioning correctly. At noon, he showed up at the house with new locks for the doors. He installed them in 45 minutes.

He is a believer. I said, "A. J., do you mind if I pray?" He said, "Yeah. Let's go to the Father together." Father, we prayed, thanking You for always being on time. You make a way when we think there is no way. Thank You for being so good and so ever-present.

In Jesus' name. Amen.

ONE MORE DAY

This is the day the Lord has made; We will rejoice and be glad in it. ~ Ps. 118:24 (NKJV)

Thank You, Father, for one more day. Strengthen me to do Your will today. I see the beauty all around me. My heart overflows with joy. I see You, Father, today. The sun, the sky, the trees, the snow, the animals scampering, trying to find food and shelter, the calmness that embraces the day, the peace that is in my heart, the feeling of serenity, the sense of belonging, the assurance of my heavenly Father's almighty hand holding everything. I know that nothing is impossible when You hold me. All my blessings are guaranteed for one more day. Thank You, Father.

In the name of Jesus. Amen.

PAINLESS KNEES

Heal me, O Lord, and I shall be healed; Save me, and I shall be saved, For You are my praise. ~ Jer. 17:14 (NKJV)

Father, I thank You for a wonderful night's rest. Thank You for blessing me from the moment that You lifted my head this morning until this present moment. Father, last night my knees ached for a moment. Thank You for keeping my knees from being stiff and uncomfortable this morning. Thank You, God. You anointed my knees with the healing balm of Gilead. Thank You for watching over me. I praise Your name, God. It was a fantastic night of relaxation and total sleep. When You woke me up this morning, I felt like a new person. You got me up on my feet, and the pain in my knees was at its best; a 1 or 2 on the Pain Scale.

Thank You, God, for knees that are not painful when I walk. Thank You for the anointing and the healing. Thank You for being You.

In Jesus' name, I pray. Amen.

PLEADING THE BLOOD OF JESUS

and by Him to reconcile all things to Himself, by Him, whether things on earth or things in heaven, having made peace through the blood of His cross. ~ Col. 1:20 (NKJV)

Father, in the name of Jesus, I plead the blood of Jesus over the family of the 14-year-old youth who was so troubled that he took the lives of 4 and hurt 30 people today. The people of the world seem to be disconnected from the realities of life. They will follow any wicked, evil, inhuman spirit that Satan releases. They appear to think that they can dissuade Satan alone. They forget to plead the blood of Jesus over life issues. Some believe they are powerful enough to fight him without invoking the name of Jesus.

You, Father, have all the power, strength, wisdom, and understanding. Our strength is weak, our wisdom is minuscule, and our power and knowledge are finite. We cannot do anything without calling on You, Father God. I plead the blood of Jesus over every youth who feels they are not who they want to be. I plead the blood of Jesus over every school-age child, every teacher, all school personnel, every troubled youth, and every adult. I plead the blood of Jesus over every form of evil, wickedness, thoughts, and deeds. I pray for the safety of every child of God. Father, keep me safe as I travel through this wilderness.

In the name of Jesus. Amen.

SURROUNDING GOD

You have hedged me behind and before, And laid Your hand upon me. Such knowledge is too wonderful for me; It is high, I cannot attain it.
~ Ps. 139:5-6 (NKJV)

Abounding God, of all that is above and below, all Your children acknowledge how great and wonderful You are. When I think of Your power, I stand in amazement at how loving You are to Your creation. You surround us every day, all day, and are constantly protecting, guiding, comforting, holding, chastising, speaking, loving, doing Your Will in and through me, it's incomprehensible. I just cannot keep it to myself. Knowing that You surround me gives me a feeling of freedom.

In the name of Jesus. Amen.

THE BALM OF GILEAD

For God is my witness, whom I serve [a] with my spirit in the gospel of His Son, that without ceasing I make mention of you always in my prayers, ~ Rom. 1:9 (NKJV)

Father, I know that You are the *healer*, Savior, *sustainer*, and *keeper* of all Your children. Thank You for being with Joyce and her two daughters. Both are being cared for by the ICU staff at Howard County Medical Center. Father, I thank You for blessing them with healing that is forthcoming. I thank You for being with this mother who goes from one room to the next, checking on her children.

Father, please let the healing balm of Gilead flow on each of them from the top of their heads to the soles of their feet. Father, I know You can and I know You will heal them physically, mentally, emotionally, and spiritually.

In the name of Jesus. Amen.

THE BATTLE IS OVER

For by Him all things were created that are in heaven and that are on earth, visible and invisible, whether thrones or dominions or principalities or powers. All things were created through Him and for Him. ~ Col. 1:16 (NKJV)

God of heaven and earth, *author* of our faith, *deliverer* and *ruler* of humankind. Your children are calling You today for a breakthrough. Some are trying to climb the ladder to rise above their situation; others are trying to heal their bodies. Some of Your children are accepting whatever is being told to them without seeking Your Council. The oppressor is trying to steal the joy that Your children have in their hearts.

Some people are unsure of where the mysterious issues originate. They are fearful of calling on the name of Jesus. They do not know that You are in every battle with Your children. They need to know that when You show up, the battle is over. Peace abounds when You are called upon.

I am an example of You showing up. I call upon You because I know that when You are called upon, You answer. Thank You, Father.

In the name of Jesus. Amen.

THE STORM IS ALMOST OVER

You will keep him in perfect peace, Whose mind is stayed on You, Because he trusts in You. ~ Isa. 26:3 (NKJV)

Father, the storms continue to rage in my son's and his friend's lives. I know, God, that the storms don't always last and that there is a bright side. I trust You, God. I pray that their faith and trust in You increase to the level where they can move, resting assured that You are with them even when it seems hopeless. I tell them that You are a *deliverer* to those who want to be delivered. You will deliver them and will put them all on the right track. Father, You promised that You will be with us always, and You let us know that every soul belongs to You.

Father, help us all to realize that we are one in the Spirit and one in You, and the storms will continue in our lives. If we look, we will see the sun peeking through the clouds. But through faith in You, we will see the sunshine and give You praise. The storms come only to teach us to have faith in You. Father; the storm is almost over.

In Jesus' name, Amen.

THE STORMS OF LIFE

God is our refuge and strength, A very present help in trouble.
~ Ps. 46:1 (NKJV)

God of strength and refuge, You have been my *helper* in ages past. You are all I need to get by in this wilderness: my *shelter* in the storm, *anchor* in the ocean, *guide* in the maze of life, *parachute* in the air, and a *hiding place* when the enemy is seeking to destroy me. You are my *protector* when others are trying to kill me, food when I'm hungry, water when I'm thirsty, oxygen when I can't breathe, my vision when I can't see, and the *one who* carries me when I can't walk. You are with me through the storms of life. Thank You, God.

In Jesus' name. Amen.

UNEXPECTED CONSEQUENCES

I again saw under the sun that the race is not to the swift and the battle is not to the strong, and neither is bread to the wise nor riches to those of intelligence and understanding nor favor to men of ability; but time and chance overtake them all. ~ Eccles. 9:11 (AMP)

Healing God of the universe, thank You for a cloudy morning. I bring before You, dear God, my cousin Francis. She was just informed yesterday that they would be preparing her for dialysis this week, and within a few days, the dialysis process would begin. Father, she is distraught. She expected this process to start in October. Lord, I know that You are in absolute control. I know that You hold her in the palm of Your hand, she is Yours, and You know all about her condition as well as what she is going through.

Father, I pray for Your grace and mercy for her. Her fears and doubts increase her anxiety. Strengthen her so that she may entirely depend on You. I love You, Lord, and I know that You know what's best for all. Our trust in You wavers sometimes. Father, I know that You'll see her through. You have been with her for 80 years, and there have been many dangers and snares, numerous surgical procedures, and various illnesses, but You are an *on-time* God. I've learned throughout the years, Father, to trust in You and to depend on Your *word*. There is no other way to live. Thank You, *healing* God, for clarity and understanding.

In Jesus' name. Amen.

YOUR WILL OR GOD'S WILL

For you [who are born-again have been reborn from above—spiritually transformed, renewed, sanctified and] are all children of God [set apart for His purpose with full rights and privileges] through faith in Christ Jesus. ~ Gal. 3:26 (AMP)

Father, thank You for Your trust in us to decide to do Your *will*. I pray for those who would rather live in their will than Your *will*. I have learned through the years that Your *will* is the only way to true happiness. We can try our way, but often it's not successful. We lose time, energy, focus, hope, faith, and get disappointed and angry, all because we did not listen to that still, soft, quiet voice.

Father, help us to get ourselves out of the way. Let us want to live in Your *will*. Open our minds to receive and believe that living in Your *will* is the only way that we can live.

In Jesus' name, I pray. Amen.

6

SEE YOU WHEN I GET HOME

A DEAR FRIEND WHO HAS GONE HOME

But the end of all things is at hand; therefore be serious and watchful in your prayers. ~ 1 Pet. 4:7 (NKJV)

Father God, thank You for the life of my dear friend, Marion Edward Pearson, whom I have known since birth. He was a friend of my cousin, Mary. He attended Olive Hill High School in Morganton, NC. He and his brother were always gentlemen. They always dressed well for every occasion. You've never seen them playing any sports.

I knew his wife from Texas, and I was familiar with their two children. Over the years, we remained in contact; whenever I went home to Morganton, I visited the Pearson's. His wife is a very charming lady. They were a lovely couple, good church-going people. They were not people who meddled in other people's business nor carried tales. They were just God-fearing people who loved the Lord and wanted to be loved and respected, and gave love and respect to others. They will be missed by the community and in their home church. I thank You, God, for their lives. Thank You for the history that we shared and the bond that grew between our families. Thank You for their children, their grandchildren, and their great-grandchildren who are still growing in Your grace.

In Jesus' name, I pray. Amen.

A FRIEND CALLED TO REST FROM HIS LABORS

Then I heard a voice from heaven saying to me, "Write: 'Blessed are the dead who die in the Lord from now on.' " "Yes," says the Spirit, "that they may rest from their labors, and their works follow them."
~ Rev. 14:13 (NKJV)

Lord, You Who love us, bless us repeatedly, and decide when it's time to rest, have called our friend, Avon Evans, home. Father, he is a good man. He believes and trusts You. Even now, he knows that You will carry him through this valley of the shadow of death. He has no fear, for he knows that his Heavenly Father will always be with him. Thank You for his life here with us for a brief time. I know that we will see him when I get home. Thank You for the now and the hope for years to come.

In Jesus' name. Amen.

A SCHOOLMATE CALLED TO ETERNAL REST

Blessed are those who mourn, For they shall be comforted.
~ Matt. 5:4 (NKJV)

Father God, thank You for a young man who has been so helpful to my younger sister. Thank You for his life and his support of her. He would shop, run errands, and even cook for her. They were real friends. They were like sisters and brothers. I thank You for his life and his time.

You called her home 36 months ago. You called him home yesterday. I know there will be quite a reunion when they meet on Heaven's shore. Thank You for their time in the wilderness with us. They both taught us how to live. Thank You, God, for this schoolmate who is being reunited with Olive Hill students, teachers, and friends from Burke County, NC. Ease the family's sorrow, Father, as they go through their grief.

In Jesus' name, I pray. Amen.

A SIX-MONTH-OLD BABY

This is my comfort in my affliction, For Your word has given me life.
~ Ps. 119:50 (NKJV)

Creative, *holy, righteous* God, I'm bringing before You this evening a family who lost their six-month-old baby. We ask for the blessings of love, understanding, and care for the parents of the six-month-old baby. Empower, O God, the siblings of the baby to remember the gift that God placed with the family for a brief time. Let them know, God, that You are the *giver of life,* as well as the *one who* takes life on earth.

You call us home when You decide it's time to go home. Fill their minds and hearts with memories of togetherness: the baby trying to talk, sharing hugs and kisses, and learning to crawl and sit up. Do help them remember family times. Do not let the sorrow over the loss of the baby overwhelm them.

Teach the parents, O God, to slow down and not be so project-oriented, and forget a child who may be sleeping in the car. Let us remember that the winters are too cold and the summers too hot to leave any child in the vehicle unattended for any length of time. We pray this loss will not cause separation, guilt, or anger to overwhelm the family and destroy their family unit.

Father, now let Your love, forgiveness, comfort, grace, and mercy encompass them as they move forward loving each other, loving what they have as well as loving what they had. Let them remember Your grace and Your mercy.

In Jesus' name, we pray, Amen.

A YOUNGER BROTHER CALLED HOME

because of the hope which is laid up for you in heaven, of which you
heard before in the word of the truth of the gospel, which has come to you,
as it has also in all the world, and is bringing forth fruit, as it is also
among you since the day you heard and knew the grace of God in truth;
~ Col. 1:5-6 (NKJV)

Gracious and loving God of the universe, thank You for siblings. Thank You, God, for the time that You allowed us to grow up together. Thank You for my parents, who struggled with us, educated and prayed with us. Thank You for their faithfulness as they showed us how to be men and women. How to trust in the Triune God for everything. They told us that through sickness or in health, through pain or sorrow, through whatever life gives us, we are to remember that You are in control. They also informed us that You, God, make no mistakes.

There is no order in the way You call Your children home or allow us to live long. I thank You, Father, for my younger brother. I thank You as I've watched him grow up and become the man that I believe You would have him be. I thank You, God, for allowing him to have an older brother who taught him about life. Thank You for his faithfulness, obedience, love of family, and love for You. Thank You for allowing me to see how he has led his children to faith in You.

You have now called him, O God, from his laborers to his eternal rest. I know he's happy, he sees our grandparents, our parents, and some friends who are already with You. I can see the smile on his face as he looked for others that he knew. Thank You for the time we had together, dear God. Thank You for the journey that is yet ahead for both of us, though in different places. One day, we will be reunited.

In Jesus' name I pray. Amen.

CALLED HOME WHILE WORKING

For by grace you have been saved through faith, and that not of your-selves; it is the gift of God, not of works, lest anyone should boast.
~ Eph. 2:8-9 (NKJV)

Father God, in the name of Jesus, I come before You this evening, thankful for Brother Butler. A man of God, a great husband, a good fa-ther, and truly a Christian man who lived a Christian life. While on his journey, he not only loved to talk about You and Your goodness, but he also tried to live the life that You would have him live.

On Saturday morning, dear God, You called him home. The tem-perature on Saturday was 101. This is a very hot day. Father, I know that You, *who* love us and created the beauty that surrounds us, hold everything in Your heart and bosom. Though the sun is shining and the temperature's high, You pluck Your flowers whenever and wherever You choose. You saw Brother Butler taking care of that which You have cre-ated, a beautiful lawn for his enjoyment. Father, You called him home to rest from his labor.

We thank You, God, for those who take care of creation. We belong to You, we are Yours; do with us, Lord, what You will.

In the name of Jesus. Amen.

DIVINE APPOINTMENT

as His divine power has given to us all things that pertain to life and godliness, through the knowledge of Him who called us by glory and virtue, by which have been given to us exceedingly great and precious promises, that through these you may be partakers of the divine nature, having escaped the corruption that is in the world through lust.
~ 2 Pet. 1:3-4 (NKJV)

God of the universe, thank You for the life of a dear friend who has labored in Your vineyard for years. She is the helpmate of one of Your *proclaimers*, who You allowed to rise to the office of Bishop of the AME Church Conference. She was a dutiful wife. She was a loving, caring, protective, wholesome mother of two children whom You gave to them. She worked diligently by the Bishop's side. She worked with the women in the church as well as the men and children. It didn't matter the age; she always had a *word* from You to offer to souls who were ready to receive. She's been swamped, God, and the storms that raged in her life sometimes came so fast that before she began to struggle with them, You cleared them away. She knew You to be a great God, and the territory that You gave to her was never too large. She labored well, she labored long, and she labored hard, a true woman of God.

I learned, O God, this morning at 8:45 that You called her home to rest from her laborers and to receive her reward. Thank You, God, for her presence. African American women of every denomination will miss her. Father, You set up a divine appointment for her. She kept the appointment, and now she is home. I see the smile on her face as she walks around heaven, greeting those who are already there. I imagine her sitting down and having a conversation with the Saints of old and those who are in the heavenly council. Earth truly has no sorrow that Heaven cannot heal.

There are mixed feelings of joy and sorrow. Sorrow because she's gone, yet joy because she's received her reward. Thank You, God, for her journey. I know that I will see her again when I get home. Thank You for the memory. Thank You for her service.

In Jesus' name, I pray. Amen.

HOLD MY HAND

For where two or three are gathered together in My name, I am there in the midst of them." ~ Matt. 18:20 (NKJV)

Dear *ever-present* Father, thank you for the family gatherings and for being present at the bedside of a loved one as they transition to their new heavenly home.

Thank You for children, grandchildren, siblings, nieces, nephews, cousins, in-laws, out-laws, school friends, and college friends, all gathered around the bedside praying. Thank You for these same people, sharing stories of yesteryear, memories flooding their souls as they listen to the breathing pattern, as they included their loved one, as they let her know that everything was going to be alright. They assured her that they loved each other and would take care of one another.

Thank You, God, for allowing us to have these precious moments together, knowing that You are with us in the midst. Thank You for guiding us to hold hands, cry, laugh, and be with Robin these last moments on this side of Jordan.

Thank You, Father, for being with us even as we go through the valley of the shadow of death. You were with us then, and You are with us now. Thank You for the assurance of holding our hands while we run this race.

In Jesus' name. Amen.

NO MORE SUFFERING

For it is better, if it is the will of God, to suffer for doing good than for doing evil. ~ 1 Pet. 3:17 (NKJV)

God of life in this valley and God of eternal life in the place where we were given citizenship before the earth stood. Thank You for the journey in the wilderness. Thank You for all the mountains, the valleys, and the struggles that You brought us through.

Thank You for knowing when we are tired of struggles and ready to come home. Your grace and mercy have surrounded us all our lives. Every problem we have ever had, You always had the solution.

Thank You for gently taking Robin home today. Her family members, including all her siblings, their spouses, children, and grandchildren, came from Canada, Florida, North Carolina, and South Carolina to share stories and say their final goodbyes. Her children, their spouses and children, and her only grandson also said their goodbyes.

There were tears of pain over her leaving, tears of joy because of memories, tears of release because of suffering, hospital visits, nose bleeds, transfusions, clinical studies, treatments, consultations, and doctors' visits, are now all over. As they stood around her bedside, You gently beckoned her to come on home. Her leaving was as she lived: a peaceful, unencumbered, gentle spirit not prone to worry over issues that would arise in life. She trusted in You, God. Robin believed that things would work out if we trusted you. She knew that You are in control of Your world and Your people. She knew that nothing was as bad as it may seem. Thank You, God, for Robins' faith in You.

In the name of Jesus, I pray. Amen.

RAYMOND FIELDS, 90 YEARS + 11 MONTHS

to an inheritance incorruptible and undefiled and that does not fade away, reserved in heaven for you, ~ 1 Pet. 1:4 (NKJV)

Lord God of all, thank You for the life of our brother, Raymond Fields, a quiet man of high principles and moral turpitude. One who spoke the truth to power. A child of Yours who is a believer. He trusts You to resolve any problematic issues. He always wanted to think before he spoke. A man of peace, courage, and honor. He loves his family. He was a faithful grandfather who tenderly cared for his grandchildren. They have been his companions since his wife of 40+ years died 18 months ago.

He loves You, Lord. He followed Your precepts. Thank You, Father, for his humor. He made everyone feel special. Our brother was always helping others. Thank You, Father, for putting the goodness of God into him.

He is with You, at home now. Peace and Joy, contentment and love, no more illness or pain, no more sorrow, and no more wilderness, just eternal rest from his labors. He is smiling and happy with You and his family there. Thank You for his smile. Thank You for 90 years + 11 months on this side of Jordan. He has been a good and faithful servant. Thank You for his journey.

In the name of Jesus. Amen.

SHE WENT HOME

And if I go and prepare a place for you, I will come back again and I will take you to Myself, so that where I am you may be also.
~ John 14:3 (AMP)

Father, thank You for my friend, my colleague, a true woman of God. She has been a Preacher of the *word* of God in the United States.

This preacher woman has been on the battlefield for the Lord for 62 years. She has never been ashamed of the Gospel of Jesus Christ. A true warrior for the downtrodden and those who were in need. She has exemplified You repeatedly, Father. She opened her home to anyone who needed shelter. She provided food and clothing for many of her flock who were in need. She taught them how to trust and wait for You. She preached that You had to believe that God would make a way. We must wait; while waiting, we must be doing something.

Her faith and example were strong, and her living was not in vain. Her love for humankind was bold. She dared to speak out against doing ungodly things. You could hear her saying, "God would not be pleased with what you are doing." She has encouraged and worked with many clergywomen and men. She joined many clergy in supporting economic, healthcare, justice, and equality for all Your people.

Today, Father, I was informed that my friend, colleague, and Your child, Rev. Dr. Alfreda Lynette Wiggins, has been called home to rest. Father God, I thank You for my sister in Christ. I thank You for her example and the life that she lived in You. I'll see her when I get home.

In Jesus' name, I pray. Amen.

CONCLUSION

I believe that after reviewing these prayers for everything every day, the reader will have a clear idea of the meaning of the scriptures:

but we will give ourselves continually to prayer and to the ministry of the word." ~ Acts 6:4 (NKJV)

rejoicing in hope, patient in tribulation, continuing steadfastly in prayer; ~ Rom. 12:12 (NKJV)

Be anxious for nothing, but in everything by prayer and supplication, with thanksgiving, let your requests be made known to God; ~ Phil. 4:6 (NKJV)

It is our bounding duty to take everything to God in prayer. Our children, neighbors, strangers, United States, foreign countries, all peoples, auto accidents, tornadoes, hurricanes, storms, weather conditions, floods, brutality, churches, conferences, all gatherings, economy, financial woes, hospitals, medical professionals, colleges, schools, people stranded in airports, air, land and sea accidents, the list is infinite.

There is a profound sense of joy and comfort that comes with communicating with God. He is our source, our strength, our power. He is in control of this universe. He will fix it in His time. We must go to Him, pray, and release. It is our faith in Him and the confidence we have in Him that we know He will take care of the problem. It may not be what we want. It will be for the betterment of all of His people.

Try taking everything to God in prayer. It will change your life.

Feel the power!

CONCLUSION

CONCLUSION

I believe that after reviewing these prayers for everything every day, the reader will have a clear idea of the meaning of the scriptures:

but we will give ourselves continually to prayer and to the ministry of the word." ~ Acts 6:4 (NKJV)

rejoicing in hope, patient in tribulation, continuing steadfastly in prayer; ~ Rom. 12:12 (NKJV)

Be anxious for nothing, but in everything by prayer and supplication, with thanksgiving, let your requests be made known to God; ~ Phil. 4:6 (NKJV)

It is our bounding duty to take everything to God in prayer. Our children, neighbors, strangers, United States, foreign countries, all peoples, auto accidents, tornadoes, hurricanes, storms, weather conditions, floods, brutality, churches, conferences, all gatherings, economy, financial woes, hospitals, medical professionals, colleges, schools, people stranded in airports, air, land and sea accidents, the list is infinite.

There is a profound sense of joy and comfort that comes with communicating with God. He is our source, our strength, our power. He is in control of this universe. He will fix it in His time. We must go to Him, pray, and release. It is our faith in Him and the confidence we have in Him that we know He will take care of the problem. It may not be what we want. It will be for the betterment of all of His people.

Try taking everything to God in prayer. It will change your life. **Feel the power!**

Resources

POWER THROUGH POWER

SUGGESTED READINGS:

My beloved sisters and brothers, I encourage you to read the Bible daily. Select a translation that you are comfortable reading.

We are under the new covenant; therefore, I recommend you read the New Testament first. Get familiar with the *word* of God.

As you read these prayers in this book, also read the scripture. Read it 2-3 times. Reflect on the *word* and understand what it means.

What is your interpretation?

Then take some time to communicate with God. Pray to Him. Take all your concerns to Him. The length of time that you pray is not important. God hears you. My sisters and brothers, pray to our Father. His Spirit is within you. He wants to talk to you. He is waiting to hear from you today.

RESOURCES:

New King James Version (NKJV)

King James Version (KJV)

New International Version (NIV)

Good News Translation (GNT)

Amplified Bible (AMP)

New Revised Standard Version, Anglicised (NRSVA)

POWER THROUGH PRAYER

About the Author

Rev. Dr. Barbara J. Sands is a seasoned Pastor, Spiritual Leader, and Author with over four decades of dedication to ministry and service. Born and raised in Morganton, North Carolina, she has been a guiding force within the United Methodist Church, serving as a seasoned Preacher in four congregations for over 43 years. She also served for seven years in the Administrative Office of the Baltimore-Washington Conference. Her journey has taken her across the globe, from exploring eight regions in Africa to leading seven spiritual pilgrimages to the Holy Land.

Rev. Dr. B. J. Sands received Certification in The American Registry of Radiologic Technologists in Radiology from Johns Hopkins Medical Center in Maryland and a Bachelor of Science degree in Sociology and African American Studies from Howard University in Washington, DC. She received a Master's degree in Secondary Education from Antioch Putney in Ohio and a Master's degree in Divinity from Howard University Divinity School in Washington, DC. Rev. Dr. B. J. Sands also earned a Doctorate in Sacred Theology from the Bible College and Theology Institute, building a foundation that uniquely blends faith with insight into human dignity and resilience.

In *Power Through Prayer,* Rev. Dr. B. J. Sands shares a lifetime of wisdom, drawing on her roles as a Spiritual Advisor, Life Coach, Human Rights Consultant, and Motivational Speaker. This book, dedicated to her parents, reflects her passion for uplifting others through the power of prayer.

Now embarking on "New Beginnings" at 80, Rev. Dr. Sands continues to inspire with her philosophy: "Life gets in the way of living; remember your moral authority, keep focused and move forward in faith."

Rev. Dr. B. J. Sands lives with her husband of 52 years, Rev. Dr. Douglas B. Sands, Sr., and is a proud mother, grandmother, and great-grandmother. Her work is a testament to faith, resilience, and the call to serve—proof that it is never too late to start anew.